The
Gardens

# of Japan

Helena Attlee

Photographs by **Alex Ramsay**

The Gardens of Japan

FRANCES LINCOLN LIMITED
PUBLISHERS

Frances Lincoln Limited
4 Torriano Mews
Torriano Avenue
London NW5 2RZ
www.franceslincoln.com

British Library Cataloguing in
Publication Data
A catalogue record for this book is
available from the British Library.

ISBN 978-0-7112-2971-6

Printed in China

9 8 7 6 5 4 3 2 1

PAGE 1 A Koi carp swims among
reflected branches at Tenju-an.

PAGE 2 Cherry blossom floats among
the seedheads of lotus plants (*Nelumbo
nucifera*) at Tenryu-ji.

RIGHT The boundary fence at Ginkaku-ji
is made from vertical bamboos that
seem to mirror the trunks of the trees
surrounding it.

contents

KYOTO

Toganoo,
Makinoo,
Takao

Sanzen-in *Hosen-in*
Ohara

Hiei-zan

Entsu-ji

Shoden-ji

Arashiyama
Sagano

Ryogen-in *Daisen-in*
Koto-in
Kinkaku-ji
Ryoan-ji

Ginkaku-ji

Tenryu-ji

Heian Jingu

Nanzen-ji Hojo
Murin-an   *Konchi-in*
Tenju-an
Higashiyama

Saiho-ji
Shosei-en

Katsura Rikyu

Tofuku-ji

Nishiyama

Katsuragawa

Kamogawa

JAPAN

Abashiri

Asahigawa

H o k k a i d o

Otaru
Sapporo
Obihiro
Kushiro

Muroran

Hakodate

Aomori   Hachinohe
Hirosaki

Akita   Miyako
Kamaishi

Sakata

SEA OF

Yamagata
Sendai

JAPAN

Niigata
Fukushima

Nagaoka   Wakamatsu
Koriyama

Iwaki

H
O
N
S
H
U

Kenroku-En
Kanazawa

Utsunomiya   Hitachi
Mito
Kairaku-En

Toyama
Ueda   Takasaki

Fukui
Matsumoto

Sabae
Takefu
Kofu   Tokyo   *Higashi-*
Gyoen   Choshi

OKI-SHOTO

Matsue

Adachi Museum
of Art

Biwa-
ko
Gifu

Kawasaki   Chiba
Yokohama   Mobara
Mt Fuji   Odawara   Yokosuka

Nagoya
Kyoto   Toyota
Daichi-Ji
Shizuoka

Okayama   Kobe
Toyohashi
Koraku-En   Osaka   Hamamatsu
Sakai
Matsusaka

Tsushima

Hiroshima

Kure

Ritsurin-Koen
Takamatsu

Shimonoseki
Tokushima   Wakayama

Kita-kyushu   *Suo-nada*

Matsuyama   *Shikoku*

Fukuoka

Kochi

Sasebo

Omuta

Nagasaki   Kumamoto
Suizen-Ji

K y u s h u

Kagoshima   Miyazaki

PACIFIC

OCEAN

JAPAN

0   100   200 Miles

0   100   200 Kilometres

introduction

A Monday night in early April, and Maruyama Park in central Kyoto is packed with festive crowds. The paths are lined by stalls selling whole herrings smoked in ash and served on a stick, whole barbecued squid, also on a stick, charcoal-baked yam, chocolate-coated bananas and many other less easily identified treats. The cooking food makes an exotic mixture of scents that mingles with laughter in the air, and as darkness deepens the colourful paper lanterns on the stalls are lit. What has drawn all these people out into the cool night, and what is fuelling their great good humour? The food alone could not create this festive, carefree atmosphere. No, the main attraction here is *sakura*, the blossom of the cherry trees that grow all over the park.

This week *sakura* reaches its peak, drawing thousands of people to revel in the almost ethereal beauty of the floodlit blossom and celebrate the promise of spring. Since early morning there have been tarpaulins laid out to reserve places beneath the trees. Now this sea of pale blue plastic is obscured by revellers enjoying a *hanami*, or flower festival, picnic. All life is here, beneath the raft of beautiful pink blossom and the indigo night sky. There are huge, informal groups of students, more formal ones of men in suits and women in kimonos, and intimate family groups made up of only parents and their small children. By eight o'clock it's standing room only and a couple of late arrivals must squash themselves into a niche between a tree trunk and the corner of a hedge.

It is perhaps surprising that the citizens of this intensely urban and technologically advanced country should still gather in their thousands to celebrate the blossoming of the cherry with a festival that is already 1,500 years old. However, the same acutely felt link with the natural world also draws the crowds into Japanese gardens, where they find nature condensed and brought to perfection. Trees are trained and pruned until they epitomize the very best of the trees' tree-like qualities, the finest natural landscapes are reproduced in miniature and the seasons are celebrated with spring blossom and the fiery leaves of autumn.

HISTORY

Each era of Japanese history developed its own style of garden design, but earlier styles were never discarded. Consequently, in Japanese gardens old and new are interleaved and inseparable, rather than being, as Japanese garden historian and author Teiji

Itoh puts it, 'piled up like strata in an archaeological excavation'. Although there is written, painted and even physical evidence of gardens during the Nara period of 710–94, this process of evolution and accretion really got under way during the Heian era of 794–1185. Heian-era gardens were built on the large estates of the aristocracy. Their style is defined in Japanese as *chisen shuyu teien*, which translates clumsily but rather evocatively as 'pond-spring-boating-garden'. A pond may not be a poetic concept in Western culture, but the Heian garden pond was a lovely, complex body of clear spring water decorated with rocky islands, inlets and peninsulas. The influence of Chinese culture was strong in Japan at this time and the islands in the pond were often designed to resemble the Mystic Isles of Chinese legend, where the immortals lived in perfect harmony, flying from island to island on the backs of obliging cranes.

The pond was at the heart of the garden, and of the wonderfully leisured, light-hearted and sensuous lifestyle of the aristocracy. Their boating parties were highly theatrical affairs. Guests drifted about in beautifully carved and painted boats to the accompaniment of music played by a floating orchestra. The garden was designed to be seen from the water, and visitors contemplating its beauty often felt inspired to write poetry. The complex system of ponds that still lies below the temple of Ryoan-ji in Kyoto was originally built during the Heian era.

A second strand of garden design known as the Pure Land or Paradise style reached its apotheosis in the eleventh century. Ponds were once again the core feature of gardens in this style, which were designed as earthly representations of Amida Buddha's Western Paradise. Saiho-ji, Kyoto's famous Moss Garden, began life as an earthly paradise created by the Jodo, or 'Pure Land' Buddhists.

Two very illuminating Heian-era texts have survived from the eleventh century. The first is *The Tale of Genji* (1001–1020) by Lady Murasaki Shikibu, an ex-lady-in-waiting who was perfectly placed to create an intimate vignette of courtly life. The book contains several intensely detailed descriptions of beautiful gardens, their plants and the parties that took place in them. Prince Genji, the hero, seems to express the spirit of the Heian era when he says: 'Aside from house and family, it is nature that gives me the most pleasure, the changes of the seasons, the blossoms and leaves of autumn and spring, the shifting patterns of the skies.'

The second seminal text is *Sakutei-ki*, or 'Records of Garden Making', which was written in the middle of the eleventh century by Tachibana no Toshitsuna. It is a manual of garden design that contains practical advice on every aspect of garden building. Some of the instructions would be as easy to obey today as they were in the eleventh century, while others might create some difficulty. When setting stones, for example, 'Choose a particularly splendid stone and set it as the Main Stone. Then, following the request of the first stone, set others accordingly.' This is one of several instructions regarding rocks, which were already an important feature of the garden, to be sought out on mountainsides or uncovered on riverbanks, transported, sometimes with enormous difficulty over long distances, and finally arranged in the garden with infinite care. The priests responsible for garden building in the Heian era and the Kamakura era that followed it were called *ishitateso*, or 'rock-setting priests'. They were always drawn from the lowest ranks of the priesthood because any work involving earth – be it well digging, plastering, kiln construction or garden building – was considered demeaning.

The *ishitateso* were gradually usurped by the *kawaramono*, or 'riverbed people'. In the thirteenth century the *kawaramono* were outcasts, permitted to live only on the common land beside the Katsura and Koomo Rivers, and to earn their living from jobs too menial for any other sector of society. They first found their way into gardens as manual labourers, but their role gradually changed. They were ideally placed to spot suitably shaped rocks in the river and on its banks. First they sourced the rocks and then they learned to place them. By the fifteenth century they had gained so much respect that they began to take over the work of the *ishitateso*.

The Kamakura era of 1185–1333 was a period of transition for the Japanese garden. Power shifted from the aristocracy to the warrior class and this brought the golden age of the great aristocratic garden to an end. Zen Buddhism was introduced to Japan from China and with it came a new and very much simpler aesthetic that slowly infiltrated every level of creative life. The first example of a landscape inspired by Zen Buddhism is thought to be Saiho-ji in Kyoto, built by Muso Soseki, the great Zen priest and teacher, in *c*.1334. Saiho-ji also contains the oldest known example of a dry cascade, a dynamic arrangement of rocks that suggests the flow of a great mass of water.

Most of the wonderful gardens made in Kyoto during the Heian and Kamakura eras were casually destroyed during the Onin Wars that raged from 1467 to 1477. A new style of garden emerged from the city's smouldering ruins. It was made from only rocks and sand, ingredients that were carefully combined to create a monochromatic,

highly abstract and distilled version of the natural landscape. The *kare-sansui*, or dry garden, of the Muromachi era (1393–1568) was a perfect expression of the elegant and austere Zen aesthetic. Its creators took their inspiration from the beautiful ink-and-wash landscape paintings of the Sung Dynasty that were brought back to Japan from China by Zen monks. They rendered the landscape's unpainted voids in white gravel, and its mountains in rocks with forms carefully chosen to resemble the angular brushstrokes characteristic of certain Sung-dynasty painters' technique. The most highly prized rocks came from the Kurama region near Kyoto. They were full of iron ore and the brown markings on their surfaces caused by oxidation made them particularly valuable. White gravel was easily available in Kyoto. The Higashiyama mountains on the east side of the city are composed of white granite. This breaks down with weathering and runs off the mountains in streams and rivers. The gardens composed from these elements were not made for touching or walking through. They were designed, like paintings, to be viewed from a static position. The most famous examples of *kare-sansui* are Daisen-in and Ryoan-ji.

It is often assumed that *kare-sansui* gardens were used as a focus for meditation. However, the link between the garden and the life of Zen monks was generally through maintenance rather than meditation. In Zen practice, all human activities can become a spiritual discipline. Clearing the garden of weeds or fallen leaves, or restoring a perfectly raked pattern to the gravel became an integral part of the monks' religious life.

The Momoyama period (1568–1600) saw the flowering of a new garden prototype: the tea ceremony garden. Tea drinking was synonymous with Zen, for monks traditionally drank tea to keep them alert during long periods of meditation. The new garden style could scarcely have been more different from the *kare-sansui* that preceded it. Unlike *kare-sansui*, the tea garden is specifically designed to be walked through by guests on their way to a tea ceremony. It is a place of transition between everyday existence and a more contemplative world. A narrow, twisting path, or *roji*, leads from the garden entrance to the tea house. The spaces to either side of the path are planted with a muted palette of glossy evergreen varieties which are arranged in an informal and naturalistic manner. The *roji*, or 'dewy path', is composed from stepping stones. The host always sprinkles water over the stones before guests arrive and this serves both to tell the guests that their host is ready for them and to create a pleasing atmosphere of freshness and cleanliness. The designer of the tea garden uses the stepping stones as a means of controlling the speed at which a visitor passes through the garden, a

Rocks in the garden of Ishidaan at Ryogen-in. This modern garden was inspired by the ancient legend of the Mystic Isles. The tallest rock represents Mount Horai, an island in a sea of white gravel.

Uchihashi-tei, the romantically named Floating Tea House on the shore of the Misty Lake at Kenroku-en. A boat is moored in the shelter of the building.

technique that was later used to great effect in the stroll gardens of the seventeenth century. The stepping stones at the garden entrance may be quite widely spaced, but as the path approaches the tea house they are placed much closer together, compelling the visitor to slow down to a more meditative pace. Other preparations for the ceremony include the rinsing of hands and mouth in a *tsukubai*, or stone basin, that is placed beside the path. Beautiful stone lanterns are used to illuminate the *roji* at night.

Kobori Enshu (1579–1647), a feudal lord in the early Edo era, was one of Japan's greatest tea masters. He is named as the designer of many of Kyoto's most important tea ceremony gardens, but Konchi-in, a sub-temple within the monastery of Nanzen-ji, is one of the very few that can be attributed to him with absolute certainty.

The *roji* made an enormous impact on Japanese garden design. It introduced the idea of movement through the garden landscape which would be developed in the seventeenth-century stroll garden, and also the philosophy of *wabi sabi*, which teaches an appreciation of imperfection. Inside the tea house damaged or imperfectly fired tea bowls might be used, and in the garden the designer might select materials that were weathered, such as moss encrusted or otherwise marked by the patina of age. Stones had always been valued for their antiquity. The patina – or *wabi* – differs with the provenance of the stone, for the weathering of a stone on a mountainside will be entirely different from weathering by the sea. Once in the garden, the unique patina continues to evolve.

Teiji Itoh remarked that old forms and styles of Japanese gardens were never really eradicated by changing fashions. 'Old and new have shared places,' he said, 'coeval and appreciated in all periods.' The stroll gardens that evolved during the Edo era of 1600–1868 were the ultimate example of this process of accretion and accumulation. They were large, beautifully landscaped parks built for the entertainment of the *daimyo*, or feudal lords, who owned them. There is something of the Heian pond garden in their streams and stretches of water, but the stroll garden pond is usually too small to be navigated by boat. Instead, visitors find themselves on a narrow, winding path that leads them along the water's edge, over bridges and stepping stones, through groves of beautifully pruned trees, between artificial rolling hills and past tea houses and elaborate arrangements of rocks. The path is paved with stepping stones. Sometimes these are made from rough, uncut stones that are arranged at odd distances from each other so that the visitor must look down and focus his attention on the ground. At other times the stones are smooth and evenly laid, or even replaced with long, smooth stone planks, allowing the visitor to look up and take in the view that has been prepared for him. The view was very often a recreation of a famous landscape – Mount Fuji's familiar profile made in miniature, perhaps, or an imaginary scene from a famous Heian-era poem such as *The Tales of Ise*. During his walk the visitor would encounter the same view again and again, each time from a slightly different angle. There were rock arrangements, too, but they had lost their religious significance, as had the shrines and tea houses tucked away among the trees, for this was an entirely secular garden. One of Japan's finest stroll gardens is Katsura Rikyu in Kyoto.

In 1854 Japan signed a treaty with the United States, bringing two hundred years of cultural isolation to an end. This dramatic event had an enormous impact on every aspect of Japanese culture, including that of garden design. During the Meiji era of 1868–1912 a very much broader spectrum of plants began to be used and the rolling, carefully mown lawns of the English landscape garden were often incorporated into the design of new Japanese gardens. The feudal system was rapidly abolished, and almost all the palace stroll gardens made for *daimyo* during the Edo era were turned into public parks.

CLIMATE

Japan is an archipelago made up of four main islands, Hokkaido, Honshu, Shikoku and Kyushu, that stretch from the north-east to the south-west. The country covers 20 degrees of latitude, and this results in a complex climate that ranges from subtropical in the south to arctic in the extreme north. The influence of continental Asia in the west and the Pacific Ocean in the east creates very distinct seasons. Spring begins in March with the blossom of the Japanese apricot (*Prunus mume*), which is followed by the cherry blossom in early April and azaleas in May. June is the rainy season, and the persistent, drenching drizzle transforms the moss that clings to every surface in Kyoto's gardens from khaki to iridescent green. Hydrangeas and *Rhododendron indicum* burst into flower. The stifling heat of summer is followed by a brief but intense typhoon season of high winds and heavy rain. October, like April, is an immensely popular time to visit gardens. Soft light illuminates the beautiful autumn colours of maples and other carefully selected garden trees. Winter brings heavy snow to the western side of Japan, where trees and shrubs are often protected by remarkable structures built from bamboo, matting and rice fibre ropes.

The gardens in this book are arranged alphabetically, and marked on the map on page 6. The contact details of all the gardens in this book are listed in the 'Visiting Japanese Gardens' section on page 134.

A viewing window at the Adachi
Museum in Yasugi shows part of
the Dry Landscape Garden.

Adachi Museum of Art and Gardens

The Adachi Museum is surrounded by a vast modern garden that is designed to be seen entirely from inside the building, or from the viewing platform that surrounds it. Consequently, we view the garden landscape in exactly the same way as we do the paintings here: as outsiders staring into a vivid and beautifully framed scene, able to appreciate the atmosphere, technique and colours, but forbidden to feel the texture of the rocks or leaves with our hands, or the surface of the paths beneath our feet. Adachi Zenko (1899–1990) described the garden that he had created as 'a picture scroll, a living painting'. He arranged for it to be viewed from inside the museum through windows of various shapes and sizes that serve to frame it like the paintings and scrolls on the walls to either side. In this way he integrated his outstanding collection of 1,300 paintings, all from the post-Meiji period, with six different garden landscapes outside. He was particularly keen to forge a link between the landscape paintings of Taikan Yokoyama, which form the core of his collection, and the garden landscape, as he was convinced that this link would enrich his visitors' experience of the paintings.

The Adachi Museum and garden were built on the proceeds of a long and successful career, made all the more satisfying by its humble beginnings. Adachi Zenko was only fourteen when he began work, delivering charcoal in a barrow. He had to haul his load over 9½ miles/15 kilometres each morning. He had nothing but straw sandals to wear on his feet, even though the snow was often thick on the ground. He soon wondered if he might be able to sell more charcoal en route to his destination. He took to piling the barrow higher, and it wasn't long before he doubled his income. This was the beginning of a business career so successful that it allowed him to amass a huge collection of modern Japanese paintings, and made him the leading collector of the precious works of Taikan Yokoyama in the world. He opened the museum in 1970, at the age of seventy-one, and began work on the garden immediately.

Adachi took a passionate interest in gardens and garden design throughout his life. Before setting to work on the museum gardens, he travelled all over Japan to look at other important and inspiring landscapes, and to find pines and rocks for his new garden. Over eight hundred red pines (Pinus densiflora) were brought to the site of the new garden in Yasugi, along with many thousands of painstakingly selected rocks. He applied his superb visual sense to identifying the very best specimens. Hiroichi Sugihara, who worked as the garden's manager for twenty years, was particularly struck by Adachi's memory. 'What was truly astounding,' he says, 'was that he knew exactly where each and every tree and rock was in the garden.' Kinsaku Nakane, former president of Osaka's University of Art, was commissioned by Adachi to design a garden at the entrance to the museum. He was staggered by the beauty of the rocks that Adachi had collected, remarking that he didn't expect to see anything so fine again in his own lifetime.

Adachi continued to care for the garden until the day of his death at the age of ninety-one. According to Hiroichi Sugihara, he 'was not content to let the garden be and he was constantly working on it'. He would inspect the site morning and evening, and he was quick to call on the gardeners if he found anything wrong. Hiroichi Sugihara recalls an observation that Adachi made towards the end of his life about managing staff. It evokes an endearing image, for he remarked that a person who could not tell jokes was equally incapable of giving orders. 'And true to form,' Hiroichi Sugihara says, 'instead of simply ordering his staff, he would give orders interspersed with jokes, each one tailor-made for the person he was talking to. Before we knew it, we found ourselves doing exactly as he wished.'

Adachi created six very distinct areas in the garden, and he also worked to draw the surrounding landscape into his design, making the site appear very much larger than it actually is. The principal areas of the garden were given simple, descriptive names. There is the Moss Garden, where a sea of pale gravel flows between islands of moss planted with red pines. The pine trees were all imported from a mountainous site where they resisted the pull of gravity by growing at a violent angle. The gardeners replanted the trees in exactly the same way, and this gives the Moss Garden a wonderfully idiosyncratic and windswept look. Juryu-an is the name given to the peaceful garden surrounding a tea house behind the museum. The building is an imitation of Shokin-tei, one of the tea houses in the garden of Katsura Imperial Villa. The White Gravel and Pine Garden is a recreation of Taikan Yokoyama's masterpiece Hakusa Seisho ('The Beautiful Pine Beach'). Then there is the Pond Garden, surrounded by elegantly dwarfed pines, and the Kikaku-no-taki Waterfall, which tumbles down from Mount Kikaku, a natural bluff, into the Dry Landscape Garden. This Dry Landscape is the main event, the garden around which all the others revolve. It is a rolling landscape of grass and gravel set against the rocky, tree-clad bluff behind the garden. It is here that Adachi's eye for detail is vividly revealed. Every clump of clipped azalea, rock and dwarfed pine is painstakingly arranged to create the illusion of almost infinite space.

RIGHT The back wall of a *tokonoma*, or alcove, inside the Adachi Museum has been cut away to give a perfectly composed view that resembles a painting on a hanging scroll.

The rounded hull of Kobori's 'ship' at Daichi-ji encloses a pile of square treasure chests.
The undulating shape of the hedge beyond the ship suggests the waves in a rough sea.

Daichi-ji

It's quite a journey to Daichi-ji. The first train takes twenty minutes to reach Kusatsu, on the edge of Kyoto. The local train from Kusatsu to Kibukawa carries you deep into the country, where every flat patch of land without a house on it is put to use as a paddy field or a vegetable patch. In early spring the first rice crop of the year is no more than a green haze above grey water, and in the villages futons and quilts hang out to air in the sunshine. A bus that leaves Kibukawa station once an hour can drop you somewhere near Daichi-ji. Not too close, though. You still have to walk up the road and along a path that runs between the lake and the hill, but there's no hardship in that.

Daichi-ji was founded in the eighth century. Much of the complex has recently been rebuilt with money raised by the local community. The building is made from cedar, and it is still strongly scented by the new wood. A vast, black pine (*Pinus thunbergii*) has grown by the entrance of the temple for 350 years. Time and precise pruning have transformed it into a magnificent, supine dragon, its great fat belly resting on the ground.

The temple is surrounded by enclosed gardens, the most important of which is the Hourai garden outside the *shoin*, or study. It is a gravel garden almost entirely filled by one of the most complex examples of azalea topiary (*karikomi*) to be found in Japan. *Karikomi* has always been a part of the Japanese garden, but it was transformed into an exuberant art form at the end of the sixteenth century by Kobori Enshu (1579–1647), the designer of a number of gardens in the Momoyama and early Edo eras (1568–1600 and 1600–1868). He introduced the idea of creating *karikomi* on a much larger scale, using groups of clipped plants to suggest mountain landscapes, waves or forests. The *o-karikomi* (the 'o' prefix means 'large') at Daichi-ji is attributed to Kobori Enshu himself. It consists of a great number of azaleas (*Rhododendron* x *obtusum*), clipped and combined to suggest the shape of a treasure ship. The sinuous, undulating forms of the hedges turn pink with flowers in May and June. *Rhododendron* x *obtusum* can be evergreen in warm climates, but not at Daichi-ji, where the leaves are suffused with gold in autumn and flush purple in winter. Winter snow can create another wonderful effect, although falls of over 12 inches/30 centimetres can damage the delicate structure of the hedges.

The abbot of Daichi-ji maintains the garden himself. He rakes the gravel around the hedges every morning, keeping it clear of fallen leaves. Pruning is done when the azaleas finish flowering in June, and again after their growth spurt in autumn. When asked whether he uses the garden for meditation, he replies, 'No, but I feel it with my heart.'

Daisen-in

Daisen-in is surrounded on four sides by one of the most famous garden landscapes in the world. To visit it is to find yourself at the centre of a Chinese, Sung-dynasty landscape, an imaginary painted world made real. It is no coincidence that this three-dimensional painting should traditionally be attributed to Soami (1472–1525), one of the most celebrated landscape painters of his age, for his exquisite and highly detailed paintings of rural landscapes in different seasons of the year decorate the screens in the main hall. However, records show that the garden was actually laid out by Kogatu Shuko (1464–1548), who founded the temple in 1509 when he retired as abbot of Daitoku-ji. He was probably advised by Soami and assisted by *kawaramono*, the lowly riverbank workers who had by this time become highly respected garden designers. The *hojo*, or abbot's house, was completed in 1513, and the gardens that surround it were probably built over the same period.

Daisen-in floats on a glittering sea of raked gravel. The source of all this imaginary water is a cataract coursing down the craggy face of a miniature mountain set in a rocky landscape planted with clipped azaleas and dwarfed pines. The water is represented by veins of white quartz running through the vertical rocks that form the mountain. When it hits the valley floor, the cataract translates into two white gravel rivers that wind their way among islands and water-worn stones. One river flows beneath the building, emerging on its other side as a wide sea punctuated by two raked gravel pyramids. The other flows into a narrow space, where it is raked into ripples and swirling currents beneath a boat-shaped rock.

The stone boat in the southern part of the garden is said to have been part of the rock collection amassed by Ashigawa Yoshimasa (1435–90). It is one of several fine and very distinctive rocks at Daisen-in. Rocks like this could be found only after a long search on the banks of rivers or among mountain peaks, and as a result they were immensely valuable. Transporting them from the place of discovery to Kyoto was an arduous and long-winded business that sometimes involved several hundred men. This was no problem for the shoguns and princes of previous eras, but by the time Daisen-in was built Kyoto had been transformed by the Onin Wars of the mid-fifteenth century. The patronage of shoguns and princes had gone for ever and virtually all of the city's great temples and magnificent Heian estates had been burned and pillaged. After a decade of fighting, Kyoto was little more than a burnt-out shell. However, rocks do not burn and they are very difficult to steal. Consequently, abandoned temples and derelict estates became a magnificent and easily accessible source of materials for the monks who created new *kare-sansui* gardens like Daisen-in.

The water that cascades through Daisen-in may be symbolic, but the camellias, azaleas and pines that grow in the mountainous landscape are absolutely real. A Japanese white pine (*Pinus parviflora*) grows on a grassy plateau among the mountains. The white pine has shorter, denser needles than the red or black pine (*Pinus densiflora* and *P. thunbergii*), and it grows at a slightly slower rate, making it ideal for miniaturization.

The north-west corner of the garden, seen from the veranda of the abbot's house. Streaks of white quartz running through the two upright rocks at the back suggest a mountain waterfall that feeds the broad river in the foreground.

Entsu-ji

Don't visit Entsu-ji if it's raining, and don't make the journey out to Hataeda, on the northern fringes of Kyoto, when the city is shrouded in summer smog. I am surprised that the abbot doesn't close the gates to visitors in bad weather, for he is certainly strict enough to forbid professional photography when the conditions are poor. Closure would be easy to justify for Entsu-ji's garden incorporates one of the most famous and effective examples of the borrowed landscape in the history of Japanese garden design. Without its view the garden is nothing.

The temple of Entsu-ji was built in c.1678 on the site of an imperial villa belonging to Emperor Gomizuno. The rectangular space below the viewing platform is entirely covered in a deep-pile carpet of moss that is inset with a naturalistic arrangement of clipped azaleas and horizontal rocks. A dense evergreen hedge surrounds the garden, dividing it from the woods and bamboo groves that surround it. There is nothing casual about this apparently informal arrangement, for every element of the garden is part of a complex composition that extends far beyond the boundary hedge to incorporate the distant contours of Mount Hiei.

Anyone can build a garden with a fine view, but it is very much more difficult to integrate that view into your design, so that the garden seems to extend seamlessly beyond its actual boundaries to the far horizon. This technique, which came to be known as *shakkei*, is magnificently displayed at Entsu-ji. The earliest gardens to be built in this style date from the late sixteenth and early seventeenth centuries. According to Teiji Itoh, the technique of borrowing landscape was originally called *ikedori*, a word used in relation to hunting animals and meaning 'to capture alive'. This gives a much more vivid sense of the dynamic process by which the middle ground of the view has been used to bind the garden in the foreground to the distant horizon, so that Mount Hiei, a sacred place with many significant temples, which rises from the north-eastern edge of Kyoto, 4 miles/6.5 kilometres away, is drawn into the heart of the tiny garden.

The key to the composition at Entsu-ji is to be found among the cedars and Japanese cypress trees that grow beyond the garden boundary. All of the trees have had their lower branches removed so that their long, slender trunks seem to repeat the upright supports of the viewing platform. The mountain is framed between the vertical line of the bare trunks and the horizontal lines created by the camellia hedge and the foliage of the trees. The space between Entsu-ji and the mountain is covered in buildings, but these have been screened out by other trees, so that there is nothing to fragment the view or dispel the illusion that Entsu-ji and Mount Hiei form two parts of a single, uninterrupted thought.

Ginkaku-ji

Ginkaku-ji lies at the northern end of the Philosopher's Walk, a pretty path bordering a canal on the north-eastern edge of Kyoto. On a sunny spring morning the path is busy with groups of children who make their way quietly to school beneath a pearly tunnel of cherry blossom.

Ginkaku-ji was built in 1482, amid the chaos and devastation that followed the Onin Wars. The beautiful pavilion and garden were part of the retirement villa of Ashikaga Yoshimasa, the eighth shogun of the Muromachi era (1393–1568) and grandson of Yoshimitsu who built the famous Golden Pavilion. Its official name was Hagashiyama-dono, 'villa of the eastern hills', but it soon came to be known as Ginkaku-ji, 'the silver pavilion'. Some scholars insist that the name was coined because Yoshimasa planned to coat the two-storey building in silver leaf, but others are adamant that he had no such intention.

Yoshimasa lived at Ginkaku-ji until his death in 1490. He filled the villa with paintings collected over a lifetime and made it a hub for all the different arts inspired by Zen, although his personal focus was flower arranging and the tea ceremony. The impact of this eight-year period was so great that Zen culture of the late fifteenth century came to be known as Higashiyama, taking its name from the location of Yoshimasa's villa in the foothills of the Higashiyama mountains.

Yoshimasa left instructions for his villa to be converted into a temple after his death. His wishes were carried out and Ginkaku-ji became Jisho-ji, a Rinzai Zen temple. Today the two-storey pavilion is one of only two original, fifteenth-century buildings to have survived on the site. It stands on the edge of Kinkyochi, 'the brocade mirror pond', a name that vividly conveys the complexity of this convoluted network of ponds and islands linked by stone bridges and decorated with rocks, dwarfed pines and azaleas.

Many different names have been associated with the design of Ginkaku-ji. Some suggest that it was designed by Zenami, the leading *sensui karawamono* (or 'lowly riverbank worker turned garden designer') of the day, others see the hand of the painter Soami and sometimes the design is attributed to Yoshimasa himself. Yoshimasa is known to have loved the garden of Saiho-ji, and comparisons are often made between the design of the two gardens. According to Teiji Itoh, Yoshimasa's mother longed to see the garden that her son loved so much but, as a woman, she was forbidden to enter the temple precincts. Apparently, Yoshimasa imitated aspects of Saiho-ji to entertain his mother, who must by that time have been in her dotage. The pavilion itself is said to have been modelled on a building erected by Muso Soseki on the northern shore of Saiho-ji's ponds.

The gardens of both Saiho-ji and Ginkaku-ji have a two-tier layout, with a pond garden at the lower level and a steeply sloping dry garden above it. The ponds are smaller at Ginkaku-ji – much too small for the boating parties that took place at Saiho-ji – but the garden was designed to be viewed from the pavilion, or from the paths and bridges that quarter the site, revealing a slightly different landscape from every perspective.

Ginkaku-ji's most famous features are undoubtedly the unforgettable field of raked gravel that lies to the north-east of the pavilion and an extraordinary cone built from sand which is called Kogetsudai, or 'Moon Observing Platform', a possible reference to its odd, truncated shape. It is probable that Yoshimasa knew nothing of these features, for they are thought to have been added at the beginning of the Edo era (1600–1868), when the garden was restored after many decades of neglect. In this case Kogetsudai may be a retrospective reference to Yoshimasa's moon viewing parties, when guests would join him to watch the moon rising over the eastern ridge of Tsukimachiyama, 'moon waiting mountain', an event that often inspired poetry. At its apex, the full moon was reflected in the pool of the Moon Washing Cascade that descends the steep hill and falls into the lower garden.

LEFT Ginkaku-ji is famous for the extraordinary use made of white sand in the garden. This is Kogetsudai, a truncated cone.

BELOW The perfectly raked lines of gravel break into ripples around the base of this rocky island.

RIGHT Azaleas and camellias flower on the mossy slopes above the garden at Ginkaku-ji.

BELOW There are forty-eight different mosses growing in the garden. These examples are displayed under a sign reading 'The Inhabitants of Ginkaku-ji'. Among the labels on the mosses is one reading 'Very Important Moss – like VIP'.

Heian Jingu

The Shinto shrine of Heian Jingu in the East Gardens of the Imperial Palace in Kyoto was built only a little over a century ago, but it is considered one of the most important spiritual sites in Japan. Couple this with its role as a focus for Kyoto's civic pride, surround it with a late nineteenth-century garden designed and planted to celebrate every season of the year, and you will begin to understand why the place is generally so crowded.

In 1895 Kyoto celebrated the 1,100th anniversary of its foundation by Emperor Kammu as the Heian capital of Japan. The city marked this important anniversary by deifying Kammu as the ancestral god of Kyoto, and then building the Heian Jingu to honour his spirit. The shrine was designed as a scaled-down replica of Chodo-in, the greatest building in the ancient Heian capital. The gardens that surround it on three sides also take their inspiration from the wonderfully elaborate pond and island gardens designed from 794 to 1185 for the Heian aristocracy. However, the garden's designer, Ogawa Jihei, combined the traditional features described in Heian literature with a very modern palette of plants imported from all over the world. He had been commissioned to make a garden where people might stroll after worshipping at the Heian shrine. Consequently, it was important to create botanical interest throughout the year.

Go to Heian Jingu in the spring and you will find Minami Shin'en (the south garden) roofed with a lattice of bamboo canes that serve to support a myriad of weeping cherries (*Prunus pendula* 'Pendula'). The branches of the cherries are lightly pruned each year to create this lovely lattice. Their blossom makes a glorious pink ceiling that is reflected in the ponds and the winding, fast-moving streams that snake their way through the garden. Fallen flowers are left to form a shining pink raft on the water. Later in the season the cherry blossom will give way to the flowers of the azaleas that are threaded like plump beads along the banks of the streams. The cherries' scaffolding stays in place all year, supporting an impressive tracery of bare branches in winter.

Minami Shin'en was built at the end of the nineteenth century, but its inspiration came from the gardens of the Heian aristocracy. During the Heian era it was traditional to compose poems in the garden, and Minami Shin'en would have provided an ideal setting for a Chinese tradition imported into Japan that was known as the Feast by the Winding Stream (Kyokusi-no-en). Guests would settle down on the banks of the stream where they would soon see a cup of *saké* floating towards them on the water. Anyone who picked up the cup and drank from it was obliged to invent a poem on the spot.

Minami Shin'en is a spring garden, but Nishi Shin'en (the west garden) is at its best in early summer when the irises on the banks of the pond are in full bloom, and herons pick their way through the flowers, or stand motionless in the water, searching for fish among the lotus leaves. A small tea house nestles among the trees at the pond's far end.

The middle garden, Naka Shin'en, contains *sawatari-ishi*, 'the steps across the marsh', which are one of Heian Jingu's most famous features. The stepping stones are made from the foundation stones for the piers of Sanjo Ohashi and Gojo Ohashi, important bridges in the centre of Kyoto. The stones are arranged in an extraordinarily intricate pattern that makes it quite impossible to hurry across the water. In summer, drifts of *Iris laevigata*, the Japanese iris, bloom beside the pond.

Higashi Shin'en (the east garden) was not built until 1910. Here the wooded Higashiyama hills create the backdrop to a large pond that is lined with weeping cherries and beautifully pruned pines, their branches reaching out across the water. A winding path leads along the rocky shore towards the covered bridge that spans the far end of the pond. In the temple on the far side of the water a wedding is taking place. Women linger on the viewing platform outside, their beautiful kimonos reflected in the pond, where a kingfisher skims like an iridescent blue dart across the water.

RIGHT Weeping cherries create a wonderful ceiling of blossom over Minami Shin'en, the south garden at Heian Jingu. The canes stay in place all year, a lovely sight in winter when their intricate pattern is seen against a blue sky.

BELOW *Sawatari-ishi* or 'steps across the marsh', a complex arrangement of stepping stones in Naka Shin'en, the middle garden.

OVERLEAF
LEFT Wedding ceremonies often take place in this beautiful pavilion on the edge of the pond in Higashi Shin'en, the east garden.

CENTRE Weeping cherry trees surround the pond in the east garden.

RIGHT A young heron poised to spear fish and frogs in the shallow water on the pond's edge.

Higashi-Gyoen
The east gardens of the Imperial Palace, Tokyo

Skyscrapers jostle to the very edge of the moat that once surrounded a vast, Edo-era castle in the heart of Tokyo. From 1590 to 1868 the castle was inhabited by the Tokugawa shoguns who systematically enlarged and improved it, so that by 1636 it was already the largest castle in Japan. Seven keeps, eight defence towers, ten gates and a magnificent stone wall surround the castle, but this was not defence enough against the fires that repeatedly ravaged the wooden buildings, destroying them again and again. Eventually rebuilding was abandoned and in 1960 the Cabinet decided to make a garden on Honmaru, land once occupied by the principal compound of the castle, and Ninomaru, the second compound, which was outside the principal compound and served as a meeting place for the shogun and his feudal lords. The garden was opened to the public in 1968. The rest of the vast site forms part of the private grounds of the Imperial Palace, the home of the royal family.

Join the stream of people clad in dark city clothes that pours over the bridge across the moat, and on through the Ote-mon gate into the castle precinct. Once inside you are enclosed by the waters of the moat and by several walls built from gargantuan slabs of stone. The noise of traffic dwindles and the skyscrapers recede behind a screen of tall trees.

Ninomaru is thought to be the site of a garden designed by Kobori Enshu next to a palace erected in 1630, but long since burned down. Today the site is a lovely modern stroll garden that has been laid out around a pond already on the site. A path divides the pond in two, breaching a small island at its centre. On its shores there are stunted pines and carefully placed rocks, and in spring the water is fringed by flowering cherries that extend their branches gracefully across it. Clipped azaleas form a continuous snake of a hedge to enclose the winding paths. A grove on the north-western side of the pond is made up of 260 trees donated by every prefecture in Japan.

Honmaru was originally the site of the shogun's residence and the headquarters of the shogunate. It was repeatedly destroyed by fire and today the only original structures are the Fujimi-yagura, or 'Mount Fuji viewing keep', and Fujimi-tamon, a defence tower. During the Edo era there were eleven keeps in the inner citadel, but Fujimi-yagura is the only one to survive. It is named Fujimi-yagura because it was once possible to see Mount Fuji from it. Fujimi-tamon, the defence tower, is built on the high wall overlooking Hasuike-bori, 'the lotus-growing moat'. Today Honmaru is occupied by a vast lawn and wonderfully contoured clumps of azaleas. In spring, people pour into Honmaru and settle down beneath the cherry trees to enjoy the blossom and their *hanami*, or 'flower viewing', picnics.

RIGHT The ancient ponds of Ninomaru (the second citadel) at Higashi-Gyoen, where a traditional garden was created in the 1960s.

BELOW A court official passing the massive inner walls of the castle by the guardhouse of Higashi-Gyoen, Hyakunin-bansho.

BELOW Branches covered in white
cherry blossom arch over the water in
Higashi-Gyoen's Ninomaru.

RIGHT By early June these clipped azaleas will have formed beautiful mounds of pink flowers.

OVERLEAF Cherry trees grow all over Higashi-Gyoen. Thousands of visitors flock to the garden in April for blossom viewing picnics.

Hosen-in

Hosen-in's temple garden contains a tree so ancient and august that it dominates the space, sapping attention from every other garden feature. The tree is a Japanese white pine (*Pinus parviflora*), one of the slowest-growing members of the pine family. It is said to have grown in the garden for 700 years, time enough to achieve an enormous height and girth. Never for one moment, however, has it been left to its own devices. A natural tendency to produce straight, elongated branches has been encouraged, and over the centuries it has been coaxed to create a canopy that covers the entire garden. This approach might have thrown the site into deep shade, but the branches have been consistently thinned, and so have the needles that grow on them. Consequently, clipped azaleas grow happily in the mossy space beneath the tree. The poles that once straightened the branches are still in place, but today this scaffolding serves as support rather than restraint. The garden is best viewed from inside the temple, where the building creates a perfectly proportioned frame around it.

The 700-year-old pine may have been planted when the temple was first founded by the abbot of Shorin-in. Hosen-in once served as accommodation for pilgrims, but it soon became a training temple for *shomyo*, the melodic method of chanting sacred texts practised by Tendai Buddhists. During the seventeenth century it was partially rebuilt, using timber taken from Fushimijo Castle in Kyoto. Part of the ceiling was constructed from wood soaked by the blood of 300 soldiers who had failed to defend the castle during a battle in *c.* 1600 and consequently committed *seppuku*, a gruesome form of suicide reserved for samurai. The bloodstains are still thought to be visible on parts of the ceiling.

It is impossible to hurry a visit to Hosen-in. First you must take your place on the tatami mats that line the temple floor. Then you must drink the green tea that is offered to every visitor. As you drink you will gaze through the sculpted branches of the pine tree, through the straight stems of the bamboo grove beyond it to the mountains that enclose Ohara on all sides. Soon you will start to notice people putting their ears to two hollow bamboo canes that emerge from the decorative wooden framework beside the temple veranda. If you imitate them, you will hear a lovely, ringing sound issuing from the canes. This is the *suikinkutsu*, a device constructed from an earthenware pot with a small hole in the bottom of it. The pot has been turned upside down and sunk deep into the ground beneath a *tsukubai*, or water basin. Water drips into the pot through the small hole and falls into a shallow pool of water inside it. The splash that it makes reverberates inside the pot, creating a musical, bell-like sound.

Sturdy wooden posts support the carefully trained, snaking branches of Hosen-in's famous white pine. After seven centuries the tree has reached a height of 11m/36ft and it is 14m/46ft wide.

PREVIOUS PAGES An exquisitely framed view across the garden to the mountains can be glimpsed through the grey-green stems of the bamboo grove beyond Hosen-in's garden.

LEFT The crown of Hosen-in's magnificent white pine has been pruned over the centuries to resemble the summit of Mount Fuji.

BELOW *Edgeworthia chrysantha* 'Red Dragon' (the paper bush) grows beside the *tsukubai*, or stone basin, where a decorative china ball floats. The beautiful fragrance of the flowers wafts into the temple building at Hosen-in in Ohara.

BELOW RIGHT The ladle laid on a bamboo rack on the edge of the *tsukubai* is used by visitors to cleanse their faces, hands and mouths before they enter the tea house that stands beside Hosen-in.

Kairaku-en

The highlight of the year at Kairaku-en comes in early spring when 3,000 Japanese plums (*Prunus mume,* more correctly known as the Japanese apricot) of 100 different varieties break into blossom and fill the air with their delicate scent. The sheer beauty of this spectacle has earned Kairaku-en a place among the *Sanmei-en,* 'the three finest gardens of Japan'. Thousands of visitors flock to the garden between 20 February and 31 March for *hanami,* the blossom viewing festival. The origin of *hanami* can be traced back to the ninth or tenth centuries when people first began to gather together in order to enjoy the plum blossom.

Kairaku-en's plums are its most important feature but there is a dispute about their origins. Some people say that they were planted by Tokugawa Nariaki, ruler of Mito, for a purely practical purpose. By 1829 he is said to have been increasingly anxious about the European and American ships that were now a constant presence off the coast of Japan, and to have been convinced that an invasion was being planned. He selected an ideal site in full sun, high above Lake Senba, and planted 1,000 plum trees on it. This was long-term planning, for he intended to use the plums as a food supply for the Japanese soldiers who would defend the country against invasion. Other sources say that Nariaki stumbled across the garden site when travelling through his fiefdom and found the views from it so beautiful that he was determined to build a garden there. In this version he spent the next eight years nurturing and grafting the enormous collection of plum trees that he had tracked down in all the neighbouring fiefdoms. By 1841 he was ready to begin building Kairaku-en, 'the garden of shared pleasures'. As the name suggests, his intention was always to open it as a public park for the people of Mito, a very unusual idea at that time. By 1842 it was complete.

Tokugawa Nariaki's plum trees were used to create the Plum Forest that has always been the most important feature of the park. The 'Japanese' plum was actually introduced into Japan from China, although it is thought that isolated, wild populations already grew in Kyushu. It blooms between mid-February and mid-March and its delicate white, pink or red blossoms are often seen against a background of deep snow. Its fruit, *umeboshi,* is very much sourer than that of a western plum tree and is most often used to make pickled plums that are eaten with rice. It is also used to flavour *shochu,* a spirit distilled from rice or potatoes.

The plum carries a huge cultural cargo in Japan. The combination of pine (*matsu*), bamboo (*take*) and plum (*ume*) symbolizes good luck for the New Year. The trio are also used to make comparisons. Instead of describing something as 'great', 'greater' or 'greatest', the Japanese would say *ume* (great), *take* (greater) or *matsu* (greatest).

The plum flowers so early in the year that it is always seen as the herald of spring. The beauty of its blossom has inspired Japanese poets ever since the eighth century, and in the seventeenth century Matsuo Basho (1644–94) dedicated several haiku to it:

Scent of plum blossom
　　On a misty mountain path
　　A big rising sun.

And at the end of the eighteenth century Koboyashi wrote:

Great moon
　　wrapped in plum scent
　　all mine.

Some of the original plum trees at Kairaku-en have been replaced, but many of them are a considerable age. Each tree has been assiduously pruned to create a wonderfully contorted framework of branches that are now propped up by wooden stays. Part of the trees' great beauty lies in the contrast between the gnarled and sooty bark of their trunks and the fresh, almost luminous blossom.

The Plum Forest is the main event at Kairaku-en, but the park contains many other features. A three-storey house stands on the edge of the plum forest. It was built as a venue of concerts and educational activities for the people of Mito, and called Kobun-tei, a name derived from an ancient Chinese verse:

Where literacy is loved
The plum blossom will open.
Where learning is prohibited
The plum blossom will close.

Ko means 'love', *bun* means 'literature' and *tei* means 'a cottage or a small house'. It can have been no coincidence that Tokugawa Nariaki chose to invite retainers over eighty years old and commoners over ninety years old to compose poems with him in the main hall of Kobun-tei.

The Togyokusen spring, whose waters are thought to be very beneficial to the eyes, rises close to Kobun-tei and visitors can often be seen filling bottles and bathing their eyes. There is also a cedar forest and a grove of different varieties of bamboo. The contrast between the shady bamboo grove and the sunlit spaces beyond it are said to impart a sense of *yin* and *yang,* 'the dual cosmic forces of the Orient'.

The view into the garden from Kobun-tei, a three-storey house that stands on the edge of the plum forest at Kairaku-en.

Katsura Rikyu

Never will you have been so manipulated or so happily enslaved as in this garden, where every step you take is still guided and controlled by Prince Toshihito (1579–1629) and his son Prince Toshitada (1619–62), its seventeenth-century owners and designers. There is only one route around the garden and it is their route. Keeping the water always on your right, you must follow a winding path that will lead you though a gorgeous, undulating landscape enriched with ponds and pine-clad islands, waterfalls, graceful bridges, mossy hills and tea houses set in elegant groves of trees.

Prince Toshihito began work on the imperial villa and its 17-acre/7-hectare garden in c.1619. On his death Katsura was abandoned. It was a decade before Prince Toshitada began to restore existing buildings, extend the villa and add several tea houses to the garden. These new buildings took their place in the developing garden landscape. Sometimes they are displayed as a focus for a view across the water, but the paths leading to them are oblique, and they seem to appear and disappear at will. Katsura is the oldest surviving Edo stroll garden and this romantic and exciting landscape took on an iconic status, becoming a blueprint for many subsequent gardens. The villa has also been a continuing source of inspiration. When Walter Gropius and Le Corbusier visited it in the early twentieth century they were astonished by its design, which they described as a model for modern architecture.

Princes Toshihito and Toshitada found inspiration for Katsura in the gardens of the Heian era (794–1185), which was generally seen as a golden age by Japan's seventeenth-century nobility. Their lives were quite different from those of the Heian aristocracy, because the Tokugawa shogunate had effectively stripped them of political power. Their only escape from this harsh reality was through art, and the poetry and literature of the Heian era.

Katsura reproduces many features from the garden landscapes depicted in *The Tale of Genji*. This Heian-era masterpiece was completed in 1020, and is often described as the earliest novel ever written. Its author, Lady Murasaki Shikibu, had served for many years in the royal court, and she expertly recreates the realities of courtly life, describing beautiful palaces and their glorious gardens in enormous detail. She gives vivid descriptions of the different species of plants flowering in the gardens, and the wonderful boating parties and entertainments that unfolded against this beautiful backdrop. The princes' friends would have been quick to recognize the imaginary landscapes of *The Tale of Genji* made real at Katsura. This recreation was made particularly potent by the fact that Murasaki had actually named Katsura as the setting for Prince Genji's imaginary palace.

A visit to Katsura is an extraordinary education in all the most potent devices of Japanese garden design. The princes were profoundly influenced by Kobori Enshu's style, although the great designer is not thought to have been directly involved in the layout and it is said that they were assisted only by expert workmen. The garden is made up of a seemingly limitless series of views that unfold sequentially as you move along the path that runs beside the ponds. At no point are you allowed an overview, and the relationship between the different landscape features and the trees, tea houses, stone lanterns and bridges is constantly changing. At one moment a tea house may be screened by a carefully placed tree, while the next moment the same tree will serve to reveal and frame it.

The most muscular and manipulative of the devices in the garden is probably the path itself, which takes a long and winding route around the ponds. It is composed of a combination of different surfaces, each one demanding different degrees of concentration. If the designer wants to focus your full attention upon a carefully framed view of a tea house across the water he will make the path from smooth gravel that can be traversed without attention. Uneven paving slabs or stepping stones serve the opposite purpose. They force you to look at the ground, distracting you from all but your most immediate surroundings. By this simple technique the designers direct our gaze as surely today as they ever did. They lift and turn our heads at will, obliging us to see the beautiful landscape unfolding around us, or to focus our attention on the tiny violets that grow in the mossy carpet at our feet. Garden writers Mark Treib and Ron Herman compare this passage from the formal, easily traversed paths to the informal, rocky surfaces to *shin-gyo-so* (formal, semi-formal, informal), a design principle used in many Japanese arts but derived from the practice of calligraphy.

'Far away, in the country village of Katsura, the reflection of the moon upon the water is clear and tranquil.' The garden was a traditional site for festivals connected with the moon and the princes were no doubt inspired by these words from *The Tale of Genji* to create several moon viewing spaces in the garden. The Geppa-ro, or 'moon-wave pavilion', is one of the tea houses Prince Toshitada added to the garden. It stands on a promontory close to the villa and it is perfectly situated for seeing the moon reflected in the water. Outside the main villa there is a bamboo veranda known as the *tsukimi-dai*, designed for one of the most beautiful points in the year, the moment when the full moon rises over the pond in August.

BELOW The Shokin-tei (Pine-lute
Pavilion) is the oldest and largest of the
four tea houses of Katsura.

RIGHT A simple wooden bridge connects the Shinsen islands in the middle of the pond at Katsura.

BELOW Sixteen bridges cross the inlets of the central pond at Katsura. This one is made to a traditional design from bundles of logs laid over a wooden frame and covered with gravel and moss.

Kenroku-en

Kenroku-en is a superb example of the large stroll gardens that became fashionable during the Edo era (1600–1868). It unfolds over 25 acres/10 hectares, a huge space that is filled with an extraordinary variety of landscape features: tea houses, ponds, streams, fountains, islands, bridges and waterfalls. There may be shrines in the garden but they are purely decorative, for this is a secular space, a palace garden devised and used only for entertainment.

There are said to be nearly 9,000 trees at Kenroku-en and over 180 different species of plants. Consequently there is entertainment to be had in every season and it's little wonder that the garden finds a place alongside Kairaku-en and Koraku-en as one of the Sanmei-en, the 'three finest gardens of Japan'. Go there for the *sakura* (cherry blossom), and you will find Kenroku-en full of tourists who have come to gaze at the blossom reflected in the Gourd Pond, the Misty Lake and the streams. At this time of year the gates are hardly ever closed as there are special night-time viewings of the *sakura* on floodlit trees. Earlier in the season the crowds pour in to see blossom in the plum grove. Here 200 trees of twenty different varieties grow from undulating, moss-covered ground. Later on the irises flower on the banks of winding streams that shine like a silver net thrown over the garden, and at the end of the year there are maples of every variety to set the place on fire with their autumn leaves. In winter the show continues with the enormous pine trees that are wrapped in remarkable, tent-like structures called *yukitsuri*. These are built each year from bamboo and rice fibre ropes. They protect the trees from the heavy winter snow that might damage or even break their brittle branches.

Kenroku-en was originally the private garden of Kanazawa Castle. It was built by several generations of the Maeda clan, the *daimyo*, or feudal lords, of Kanazawa for over three hundred years. The garden developed gradually between 1676, when Maeda Tsanori moved into the castle, and 1840. In 1759 a fire destroyed the garden and its tea houses, but in 1774 the entire site was restored by Maeda Harunaga, who also added the Emerald Waterfall and a new tea house. In 1822 water from the Tatsumi waterway was diverted into the garden. This new and copious source of water, brought to the town from a river over 10 miles/16 kilometres away, inspired Maeda Naringa to add numerous winding streams to the garden. And so Kenroku-en grew, becoming larger and more densely furnished with every generation. When the feudal system collapsed at the beginning of the Meiji period (1868–1912) Kenroku-en, like so many other palace or castle gardens, became a public park.

The name Kenroku-en was inspired by *The Chronicles of the Celebrated Luoyang Gardens*, written by the eleventh-century Chinese author Li Gefei, who defines the six horticultural graces, or 'sublime qualities', of the garden as spaciousness and seclusion, artifice and antiquity, water and panorama. Kenroku-en translates as a perfect combination (*ken-*) of all six (*-roku-*) of these qualities in one garden (*-en*), and it is known as 'the garden of six sublimities'.

Visit Kenroku-en early in the morning and you will find the gardeners hard at work. Gangs of women rake the gravel on the paths, working with meticulous care to create a clean and well-defined edge, and dusting the moss free from last night's litter of leaves and twigs. They are all identically dressed in a traditional combination of trousers, jacket and conical straw hat. Beneath the hats their heads are entirely bound in scarves. What about the men? If you want to find a male gardener at Kenroku-en, look out for a bamboo ladder propped against the trunk of a tree. Then look up and there he will be, perched on a horizontal branch at the heart of the tree. If you wonder why Japanese garden trees are so exceptionally beautiful, Kenroku-en is a good place to find out. In April the gardeners pinch out the new buds on the famous pine trees, a process known as *midoritsumi*, or 'green picking', which forces a second flush of growth. This is done slowly and carefully by hand. The new growth is slightly stunted by its late start, and this gives the tree transparency, making it possible to see the view through a beautiful screen of delicate pine needles. It can take three gardeners as many days to work over one of the big pine trees. Every tree in Kenroku-en receives this level of very individual attention. There is scarcely a young tree in the garden that is not undergoing *niwaki*, a severe training process designed to develop the tree's essential characteristics or, in the words of European *niwaki* expert Jake Hobson, 'to capture and represent what being a tree is all about'.

The old trees at Kenroku-en – and some of them are very old indeed – are nursed in their senility with the aid of props and bandages. An ancient cherry tree with only a sliver of its trunk surviving has been given a prosthetic replacement fashioned from bunches of bound bamboo that are made to sit within the carapace of the original trunk, and its scars are dressed with sacking, preserving its life until the last drop of sap runs dry.

Lafcadio Hearn, a prolific author who lived in Japan from 1890 until his premature death in 1904, invented his own explanation for the extraordinary beauty of Japanese trees:

Why should the trees be so lovely in Japan? With us a plum or cherry tree in flower is not an astonishing sight; but here it is a miracle of beauty so bewildering that, however much you may have previously read about it, the real spectacle strikes you dumb. You see no leaves, only one great filmy mist of petals. Is it that the trees have been so long domesticated and caressed by man in this land of the gods, that they have acquired souls, and strive to show their gratitude, like women loved, by making themselves more beautiful for man's sake?

OVERLEAF
LEFT The gates of Kenroku-en open very early each morning, allowing the inhabitants of Kanazawa to practise T'ai Chi in the garden before they go to work.

CENTRE One of Kenroku-en's oldest trees continues to thrive within an intricate structure of props and stays.

RIGHT A gardener uses a bamboo ladder to reach the upper branches of a pine tree. He is carefully thinning the needles – a process known as *midoritsumi*.

PREVIOUS PAGES Neagarinomatsu, the raised root pine, is one of the most dramatic specimens in Kenroku-en's magnificent collection of trees.

LEFT A uniformed gardener uses a bamboo rake to clear fallen leaves and twigs from the mossy ground at Kinkaku-ji.

BELOW Dwarfed pines grow on the islands in the foreground of the view across the pond, making the garden seem very much larger than it really is.

Kinkaku-ji

Kinkaku-ji, the Golden Pavilion, is a gilded, floating palace set in a maze of ponds and islands and encircled by densely wooded hills. This exotic and deeply romantic place was created by Ashikaga Yoshimitsu, the third of the Ashikaga shoguns, shortly before he retired in 1394. There was already a thirteenth-century building on the site called Kitayama-dono, 'villa of the northern hills', which was surrounded by a beautiful pond garden. Yoshimitsu renamed the site Rokuon-ji – Temple of the Deer Park. The Golden Pavilion that he built on the water's edge was named Shariden. Its nickname, Kinkaku, was invented on account of Yoshimitsu's plans to gild the ceilings of rooms on the third floor. The original building did not have the gilded exterior walls that it has today. In 1950, however, the pavilion was burned to the ground by an arsonist. After rebuilding, the decision was taken to make the building live up to its nickname, and the second and third storeys were covered in gold leaf set on a base of Japanese lacquer. Today the reflection of these golden walls shimmers in the milky water of Kyoko-chi, the Mirror Pond.

The Golden Pavilion is a wonderful hybrid surrounded by a beautiful mongrel of a garden. The building was inspired by a mixture of influences. The Ashigawa shoguns were avid collectors of the landscape paintings of the Chinese Sung Dynasty, which had begun to filter into Japan in the mid-thirteenth century. The style of the Golden Pavilion was inspired in part by these paintings, and in part by memories of the buildings of the Heian era (794–1185). Each of the building's three storeys is surrounded by a balcony. The garden was designed to be viewed either from these balconies or from the deck of a boat drifting across the water. The paths that wind around the ponds would originally have been used only by gardeners.

Visit Kinkaku-ji today and you will find the narrow paths packed with enormous groups of visitors. Step aside for a moment, stand on the rocky banks of the pond and look down into the water. In the shallows just beyond the shore you will find a heaving knot of Koi carp. Most of them are grey, but the tangle of moving bodies is shot through with a moving thread of gold, and another of dappled orange and white. The fishes' muscular lips explore every surface, the wooden logs that line the shore, the underside of a fallen camellia flower, the sleek surfaces of each other's bodies and the air that hangs above their pond.

In our minds Koi carp are inseparable from Japanese gardens, and yet they are not native to Japan. They are thought to have originated in eastern Asia, in the Black, Caspian and Aral Seas and in China. There are records of a third-century emperor raising carp in Japan, but their real history does not begin until the seventeenth century, when rice farmers in the Nigata Prefecture of north-west Japan started to raise grey carp to supplement their winter diets. By the end of the seventeenth century some farmers had begun to notice a few carp with striking red markings swimming among the other fish. Between 1803 and 1840 these colour mutations proliferated, and by 1880 carp breeding was a well-established hobby. So, for all their lordly presence, Koi are a relatively recent arrival in the Japanese garden.

Ashigawa Yoshimitsu inherited a Kamakura-era (1185–1333) pond garden from his predecessors at Kinkaku-ji, the Saionji Kitsune family. It is thought that he elaborated on the original structure and added more islands, carefully placed rocks and trees. The garden covers only 4½ acres/2 hectares but it is cleverly designed to seem very much larger. This has been achieved by using only small rocks and pines dwarfed by centuries of exquisitely careful pruning in the foreground of the view. The planting beyond the island at the centre of the pond is designed to blend into the background, extending the apparent boundaries of the garden as far as the distant, wooded hills.

Kinkaku-ji is the last in the line of large-scale boating-pond gardens that were so popular during the Heian and Kamakura eras, and Ashigawa Yoshimitsu may have been one of the last people to host lavish boating parties. He gathered poets, artists and Zen priests around him and made his estate the centre of Ashigawa culture. The Muromachi era lasted for two and a half centuries (1393–1568), and each period of cultural importance was named after a garden made by the shogun of the day. The end of the fourteenth century was known as the Kitayama period because of Yoshimitsu's famous Golden Pavilion on the slopes of Kyoto's Kitayama hills.

Konchi-in

Konchi-in is a sub-temple within the monastery of Nanzen-ji. It has one of the very few gardens that can be attributed with absolute certainty to Kobori Enshu (1579–1647), feudal lord, architect and almost certainly the most influential garden designer and tea master of the late Momoyama and early Edo eras (1568–1600 and 1600–1868). Kobori Enshu was employed by Suden, an eminent priest and such an important political figure that he was known as 'the prime minister in the black robe'. Suden commissioned Kobori Enshu to design the garden, new abbot's quarters, a shrine and a tea house in preparation for a visit by a shogun of the Tokugawa family. All of the building work was done between 1611 and 1632, but the shogun never materialized.

Konchi-in's garden lies to the south of a sixteenth-century *hojo*, its rooms decorated with ravishing painted screens. Below the wooden veranda, which is worn smooth by slipper-clad feet, there is a dazzling sea of white gravel. On sloping ground beyond it Kobori Enshu planted a tightly packed screen of trees, their domed canopies precisely clipped to create an undulating mass of different shades and textures of green. Late in the year this green backdrop flares up with the fiery autumn colours of maples.

Kobori Enshu placed three groups of rocks between the pale gravel stage and the dense green backdrop of trees. To left and right the rocks form the familiar, if very abstract, shapes of the crane and the turtle. It is quite easy to distinguish the triangular head and pointed flippers of the turtle emerging from an undulating sea of clipped azaleas on the eastern side of the garden. A juniper, its silver-grey trunk ancient and twisted, grows above the turtle's shell. The juniper (*Junipera chinensis*) is an *habitué* of temple gardens, where it often reaches an extraordinary age. Between the turtle and the crane there is a large, flat rock. This is a *reihaiseki*, or contemplation stone.

The building of Konchi-in's garden is well documented and among the records there is the name of a man known as Kentei. He was a *kawaramono*, one of the 'riverbed people', renowned for their extraordinary expertise in selecting and placing stones. It had taken hundreds of years for the *kawaramono* to achieve this status. In the thirteenth century they were outcasts who were permitted to live only on the narrow strip of common land beside the Katsura and Kamo rivers. They scraped a living by skinning animals and tanning their hides, jobs despised by every other class of society. The *kawaramono* first found their way into gardens as manual labourers. Gradually their job expanded, for they were well placed to source the water-torn rocks that were so highly valued in the garden. By the fifteenth century they had become so skilled at placing rocks that they began to take over the job of the *ishitateso*, or stone-setting priests, who had always designed and built gardens. By the time Konchi-in was built at the beginning of the seventeenth century, even the shoguns turned to *kawaramono* for advice on the aesthetics of gardens.

The crane's rather abstract form is to the right of Konchi-in's garden. Its beak is represented by the long, flat stone and its wing is the raised, rounded rock rising from the moss to the right of the beak.

LEFT A monkey reaches for the
moon's reflection, one of Hasegawa
Tohaku's lovely, painted screens inside
Kobori Enshu's Eight Window
Tea Room at Konchi-in

RIGHT An artfully placed camellia flower
floats on the surface of the water in a
tsukubai in the garden of Konchi-in.

BELOW An ancient juniper tree grows
above the domed stone that represents
the shell of the turtle in Tsurukame no
Niwa, Konchi-in's dry landscape garden.
The turtle's head can just be distinguished
on the right-hand side of the picture.

Koraku-en

An island garden is a lovely thing. Koraku-en unfolds across a broad sandbar in the centre of the Asahi River, which flows through Okayama. It was built in 1687 for Mitsumasa Ikeda, *daimyo* or feudal lord of Okayama under the Tokugawa shogunate. The design is attributed to Tsuda Nagatada, a samurai scholar in the service of the Mitsumasa clan. Tsuda created an extensive, Edo-era (1600–1868) stroll garden with winding paths designed to surprise the visitor at every turn with unexpected views of miniature hills, ponds, pavilions, shrines, woods, tea houses and even a Noh theatre, for Mitsumasa Ikeda was a devotee of the Noh tradition and also an accomplished actor in his own right. All of these features were originally set into arable land. The only lawns in the garden were in view of Enyo-tei, a thatched guest house on the shore of Sawa-no-ike, the largest of the garden ponds. Today Koraku-en is characterized by vast areas of open lawn introduced during the Meiji period (1868–1912).

By 1700 Koraku-en was complete and Mitsumasa Ikeda began to invite his friends to the garden. On certain days of the week, however, he threw the gates open to the citizens of Okoyama. *Daimyo* succeeded *daimyo*, and each generation built a new tea house, guest house or pavilion. All these changes were accurately recorded in paintings, diagrams and written accounts that were safely stored in the family archive, making Koraku-en one of the few Edo-era gardens with a fully documented history.

The beauty of Koraku-en made it famous almost immediately, and it is little wonder that it has been named one of 'the three finest gardens in Japan'. Tsuda Nagatada took Okayama-joi – the castle that was his patron's home – as a backdrop, and its beautiful, exotic

roofline appears unexpectedly between the trees all over the garden. In those days, visitors would have crossed the river between the castle and the garden in a boat, and there are still the remains of a landing stage. Today a bridge spans the water and visitors may choose between any number of inviting paths.

In early spring they might be drawn to the plum grove, where over a hundred trees bearing red, white, pink, single and double flowers fill the air with scent. A little later in the spring the cherries will come into flower and they will be followed by gargantuan, undulating clumps of clipped azalea. Early summer will draw visitors to the wisteria pergola and the Japanese iris beds near by. In midsummer they will find the lotus (*Nelumbo nucifera*), flowering in square beds close to Sawa-no-ike, the pond at the heart of the garden. In 1951 some of the Koraku-en lotuses are said to have germinated from 2,000-year-old lotus seed that was found in 1951 buried in peat deposits by the Kemi River in Chiba Prefecture. More square beds contain herbaceous peonies that burst into flower in April. Beyond the peony and the lotus beds there are several paddy fields, which are said to be a reminder of a time when gardened and farmed land co-existed at Koraku-en. However, many other Edo-era stroll gardens – such as Katsura Rikyu, for example – include a small paddy field as part of the layout.

Koraku-en remained in the family until 1884 and then became a public park belonging to Okayama Prefecture. In 1934 the garden was very badly damaged by floods and in 1945 it suffered heavy bombing. Thanks to the detailed written and visual information in the archives, however, a complete restoration has been possible.

View from Yuishinzan Hill across
Sawa-no-ike, the largest pond at
Koraku-en.

RIGHT Enyo-tei, with its magnificent thatched roofs, stands at the centre of the garden at Koraku-en. This building was once used to receive the daimyo on his visits to the garden.

BELOW In spring, irises flower next to *yatsuhashi*, a bridge made of staggered planks. This is a visual reference to the *Tale of Ise*, when Ariwara no Narihira and his companions come across a similar bridge with a clump of irises flowering beside it.

Koto-in

Koto-in is a small sub-temple in the Daitoku-ji complex. It was founded in *c.*1603 by Hosokawa Tadaoki (1563–1645), one of the great warriors of his age. A cobbled path leads through the damp shade of maples and bamboos that grow between the main gate and the temple. This is a serene and unremarkable space until autumn, when it is transformed by the explosive colours of leaves that seem to infuse the air with liquid gold. The path has only a short distance to cover but it complicates the journey by performing a series of dramatic dog-leg turns that force the visitor to hesitate, or even come to a complete halt, before setting off in a new direction. This technique was often used by the designers of Japanese gardens; it is an effective means of slowing visitors down and compelling them to focus their attention on a series of specific views. At Koto-in the focus is a tantalizing glimpse of the garden beyond the high, ochre wall. The path appears to end in front of a closed wooden gate, bringing the visitor to a temporary halt. Anyone continuing to move at speed would not have noticed the tiny window let into the wooden gate, or enjoyed the sense of mounting anticipation that the view through it brings.

In spring Koto-in is a study in green. The small garden behind the *hojo*, or abbot's house, is enclosed by a dense grove of towering, grey-green bamboos. Moss clothes the earth and a scattering of maples casts green shade. A moss-encrusted stone lantern creates a focal point at the centre of the garden. There is nothing to distract the eye except, perhaps, the pink of a camellia flower on a high bough.

The main garden at Koto-in is designed to be seen from the fixed point of the viewing platform. On the other side of the *hojo*, however, there is a tea garden, made to be explored on a path that winds between clumps of clipped bamboo, camellia, hornbeam and rhododendron, passes a roughly hewn *tsukubai*, or water basin, and arrives at Shoko-ken, the little tea house.

The garden seen from the viewing platform at Koto-in. The stone lantern creates a focal point at its centre, an unusual layout for a Japanese garden.

LEFT Roof tiles and charred post ends sunk into the ground create a decorative pattern at the edge of Koto-in's garden.

BELOW A string-bound rock is the universally recognized 'no-entry' sign in the Japanese garden.

Murin-an

To reach Murin-an you must leave the busy road that runs beside the Biwa Canal in eastern Kyoto and turn down a shady lane almost too narrow for modern traffic. Enter the garden and you will find the drone of cars drowned out by birdsong and the sound of running water, and the busy streets surrounding you will disappear behind trees and high walls. It is the perfect illusion: an apparently rural landscape of woods, streams and distant hills, right in the centre of the city.

Murin-an originally belonged to Yagamata Aritomo, one of the country's most eminent statesmen and soldiers, a man who had travelled to Europe to study military science and returned to Japan to become minister of war and, eventually, prime minister. The garden was built between 1890 and 1894 by Ogawa Jihei, Kyoto's most important landscape architect during the Meiji (1868–1912) and Taisho (1912–26) periods.

Murin-an belongs to the period of the Meiji restoration, when Japan's sudden contact with the West resulted in rapid modernization. The Japanese soon began to abandon their own culture and Yagamata Aritomo was one of a group of aristocrats desperate to preserve the country's garden-making tradition. The landscape that Ogawa Jihei designed takes its inspiration from the stroll gardens of the Edo period (1600–1868). However, he was unable to entirely deny the exciting influence of the West, and traditional streams and winding paths are combined with the rolling, carefully mown lawns of the English landscape garden. Ogawa Jihei's design also reflected the new naturalistic style that was characteristic of the Meiji era. It was as if, in the words of Gunter Nitschke (author of *Japanese Gardens: Right Angle and Natural Form*, one of the most important European

books to be written about the Japanese garden in the twentieth century), 'Gardens were now expected to be truthful copies of nature in its "real" form. They were no longer "nature as art", nature designed and moulded by human hands, but simply part of nature made by nature.'

This is a garden that borrows everything it needs. First there is the copious supply of water that feeds the naturalistic cascade at the far end of the garden and flows on to fill two pools and a network of streams. The water is borrowed from the Biwa Canal, but it flows out of the garden's far end and is probably never returned to source. The canal had only just been completed when Ogawa Jihei designed the garden, but he went on to make several other gardens in the surrounding area, and often used the same convenient water source. Murin-an also lays claim to the Higashiyama mountains east of Kyoto, framing this borrowed landscape in the shallow-sided bowl created by its own pine and maple trees. This vast view infuses the site with a sense of space that seems almost infinite, seeming to turn Ogawa Jihei's narrow pools and tiny streams into vast lakes linked by rivers.

A meandering path leads into the garden, sometimes crossing the stream on simple stone bridges, and sometimes winding between the slender trunks of immensely tall cypresses and red pines, beneath tree-sized pieris dripping with ghostly flowers and dark-leaved camellias. Tree roots run like swollen arteries beneath moss that covers the ground with a green skin. Mounds of clipped azaleas crowd a promontory reaching out into the water and join forces with dwarfed and contorted red pines and irises on the banks of the streams.

LEFT Water pours into Murin-an
from the Biwa Canal over an entirely
convincing naturalistic waterfall

BELOW Trees form a naturalistic
woodland on the mossy ground beside
Murin-an's pond.

RIGHT White flowers and fresh spring growth on one of the *Pieris japonica* that grow all over Murin-an's garden.

Nanzen-ji Hojo

In 1381 Nanzen-ji was declared the most important temple in Kyoto, city of temples, and for hundreds of years its abbots were the greatest Zen priests of their generation. Unfortunately, the temple's elevated status was no protection during the Onin Wars of the mid-fifteenth century, when it was burned to the ground. All the buildings on the site today date from the Momoyama period (1568–1600), and the garden is thought to have been built in c.1600.

The garden lies to the south of the *hojo*, or abbot's quarters. A long rectangle of white sand is enclosed on two sides by the verandas of the *hojo* and on the other two by the clay walls of the garden. Large and particularly characterful rocks, a red pine, carefully pruned to expose its elegant structure, clipped camellias and azaleas are arranged against the garden's back wall. They rise from an island of moss with a corrugated shore. Moss softens the edges of the rocks, lapping at their sides like water and creeping incorrigibly up the trunks of the trees. This is a linear design. Its elements are arranged against the garden's back wall. They are placed in descending order of size from left to right, a technique that creates a false perspective as you enter from the east, making the garden look much larger than it really is. When viewed from the main veranda, the garden is set against a dramatic backdrop made from the massed roofs of the temple and the wooded flank of Mount Yokakuyro Dainichisanto. In spring, cherries add their raft of blossom to the woods and in autumn the maples blaze with colour.

Over the centuries the garden has been given several poetic titles. It is often known as 'Toranokowatashi', meaning 'young tigers crossing the water'. You may gaze long and hard at the rocks in the composition and still find it hard to discern this image among them. However, other things emerge. For example, the profiles of the two largest rocks seem to echo the shape of the hill's domed summit. Look longer, and you will see how the moving light and the shadows of the trees enhance their fissured, sculpted forms.

Tigers may not be easily discernible in the garden, but the *hojo* houses some of the greatest tiger paintings of the Kano school, painted by Kano Tanyu in the mid-seventeenth century. The building is divided into rooms by golden sliding doors (*fusama*) that are decorated with tigers playing, drinking, leaping and sleeping in a heap. In other rooms the doors are painted with landscapes that seem to be an extension of the garden outside. Tortured pines grow on rocky mountainsides inhabited by wonderful animals and birds. There are cranes, monkeys, geese, hawks, a wild cat and a pheasant. In another room enormous peonies bloom in the shade of a pine. A poem by Zenkei Shibayama (1894–1974), a former abbot of Nanzen-ji, is displayed in one of the rooms, giving us a glimpse of the spiritual value of the garden and these beautiful paintings:

> Silently a flower blooms,
> In silence it falls away;
> Yet here, now at this moment at this place,
> The whole of the flower, the whole of the world is blooming.
> This is the talk of the flower, the truth of the blossom.
> The glory of eternal life is fully shining here.

Nanzen-ji *hojo*'s dry garden, looking west across the roofs of the temple. The red pine (*Pinus densiflora*) has been carefully pruned to show off its elegant structure.

LEFT Cherry blossom seen against the intricate roof of Nanzen-

BELOW The rocks in the garden of Nanzen-ji's *hojo* are carefully arranged in diminishing size from left to right

RIGHT View from the *hojo* towards one of many small gardens that surround the building.

RIGHT View from the *hojo* towards one of many small gardens that surround the building.

BELOW The magnificent *fusuma* (painted screens) inside the *hojo* were decorated in the mid-seventeenth century with birds, animals and landscapes in the Chinese style.

LEFT AND BELOW Japanese gardens depend for their impact upon immaculate maintenance. In the grounds of Nanzen-ji's *hojo* gardener-monks work hard to rake the sand and keep the mossy ground free from fallen leaves

LEFT ABOVE Highly ornamental Koi carp swim in the ponds at Ritsurin-koen. Japanese carp were originally grey, but since the mid-eighteenth century carp breeding has been a popular hobby in Japan, resulting in a magnificent array of different coloured and patterned fish.

LEFT BELOW The Engetsu-kyo, a crescent-moon bridge on Ritsurin-koen's south pond.

Ritsurin-koen is a showcase for the Japanese tradition of *niwaki*, the highly skilled art of sculpting trees. The garden's name translates as 'chestnut grove', but most of its chestnut trees were felled in 1850 to make the terrain better suited to duck shooting. By then, however, the vast garden landscape had long been dominated by pine trees. Almost a thousand pines grow on the shores of the garden's six ponds, on the sides of its thirteen miniature hills, on rocky islands and grassy plains, in the precincts of tea houses, alongside winding paths and elegant bridges. They frame views, spread their branches over water and create long, sinuous hedges.

The garden unfolds against the heavily wooded flank of Mount Shiun, and the size of the pine trees is cleverly graded to blur the division between the artificial landscape of the garden and the natural landscape of its mountain backdrop, making Ritsurin-koen seem very much larger than it really is. When you consider that the garden actually covers 185 acres/75 hectares, this illusion seems almost superfluous.

Several generations of the Takamatsu clan were responsible for the creation of Ritsurin-koen. Takatashi Ikoma, ruler of the feudal fiefdom of Takamatsu, built a villa at the foot of Mount Shiun in c. 1625. Matsudaira Yorishige made a start on the garden in 1642, creating a stroll garden in the style preferred by the *daimyo*, or feudal lords, of the early Edo era (1600–1868), and subsequent generations continued to enlarge and improve it until Matsudaira Yoritaka finally completed it in 1745. Ritsurin was in private hands for 200 years, but during the Meiji restoration of 1868–1912, when the shoguns returned power to the emperor, it was transformed into a public park.

Go to Ritsurin to meet remarkable trees. Jake Hobson, the European expert on *niwaki*, goes there to see styles of *niwaki* rarely found elsewhere in Japan, and to enjoy some trees so beautifully pruned that he defines them as the definitive examples of certain kinds of *niwaki*. You won't find better *byobumatsu*, or 'screen pines', anywhere in Japan. A *byobu* is a folding screen, often decorated with a combination of cherries, maples and ancient contorted pines. Initially, the screen artists looked to nature for their inspiration,

choosing the oldest and most weather-beaten pines that they could find as their models. Gradually these painted pines, with their cracked bark and twisted limbs, began to exert an influence in the garden, where techniques were devised to create similarly contorted specimens. Many of the *byobumatsu* at Ritsurin are very small. They are used to create false perspective within the garden, a trick that is revealed only if a heron happens to wander casually by and reveal the tree's true size.

Another very unusual type of *niwaki* at Ritsurin is known as *hakomatsu*, or 'box pine'. These are pine trees that grow very close together to create huge, sinuous hedges which Jake Hobson compares to furry green caterpillars. Beneath this smooth, verdant exterior, the hedges are formed from a knotty tangle of gnarled branches.

One of the most impressive pines in the park stands close to Kikugetsutei, or 'the moon scooping house'. This is the largest tea house in the park. It was built in 1640, but in 1745 Matsudaira Yoritaka renamed it, taking inspiration from a beautiful image in a Chinese poem of the Tang era (618–906):

I scoop up some water in my hand,
And find the moon there to greet me.

The vast tree that grows outside started life as a bonsai in a flowerpot. However, when Matsudaira Yorihiro was given it in 1832 by Shogun Tokugawa Ienari, he transplanted it into open ground. The result is a vast and extraordinary creature that seems to kneel on the gravel and fling its arms in the air.

The gardeners of Ritsurin-koen prune trees throughout the year. Neagari-goyomatsu and other important trees are attended to during the traditional spring and autumn pruning periods. The less visible specimens have to wait their turn on a rolling pruning schedule that continues throughout the year, regardless of season. The results of this very practical but somewhat unorthodox approach are absolutely spectacular.

LEFT A heron appears to mimic the trees as it stands on the banks of the Senkan-chi pond at Ritsurin-koen.

BELOW A view across Ritsurin-koen's north pond towards the Bairin bridge.

Ryoan-ji

This sparse composition of gravel and rocks is the most famous garden in Japan. It is the quintessential *kare-sansui*, a garden without water, without plants or trees. Its image is so well known that many people believe this to be the only idiom of Japanese garden design.

The garden consists of a rectangular area on the south side of the *hojo* or abbot's house. It is enclosed on two sides by a shingle-clad clay wall. The clay was boiled in oil before being used to build the wall. Over time the oil has leached out, creating intriguing black-and-grey patterns on the ochre-coloured surface. This effect is so unusual that the wall has been made a national monument in its own right. The ground is covered in pale quartzite grit. This is raked into perfectly parallel lines that run along the length of the garden, breaking into ripples when they encounter the rocks. There are fifteen rocks in the garden, arranged in groups of 5-2-3-2-3. Each group is surrounded by a tiny island of moss.

Ryoan-ji is in north-west Kyoto, on an estate that once belonged to a famous Muromachi-era (1393–1568) general called Hosokawa Katsumoto. He acquired the property in 1450. It had originally belonged to the Fujiwara clan, and at the beginning of the eleventh century Fujiwara Saneyoshi built the beautiful Heian pond garden that still lies below the temple today.

When was Ryoan-ji built? Who built it? What does it mean? There are no certainties in this garden, only questions. There are many theories about the date of the garden, but it is generally thought to have been built in 1488. By this time Kyoto had been ravaged by the Onin Wars, Hosikawa was dead and his temple had been burnt down. The Ryoan-ji temple was rebuilt and dedicated to the Rinzai sect of Zen Buddhism. There is no documentary evidence relating to the garden, but it is generally accepted that it was built at the same time. The designer's name is equally uncertain, but one of the stones has the names Kotaro and Seijiro chiselled into it. This is a unique phenomenon and research has revealed that these names belonged to two *sensui kawaramono*, riverbank workers turned gardeners. By the fifteenth century the *kawaramono* had transformed themselves from outcasts and lowly manual labourers into highly esteemed experts in garden design. It is quite possible that Kotaro and Seijiro worked alongside Zen monks to create Ryoan-ji.

A great deal has been written about the meaning of the garden. Interpretations include symbolic islands in a sea and a tigress leading her cubs across a river. Garden writer Gunter Nitschke rejects these explanations and adopts what he describes as 'a more existential approach . . . whereby the garden and its effects are simply experienced for themselves . . . I see it as an abstract composition of "natural" objects in space which is intended to induce meditation.'

Visit Ryoan-ji early, before the crowds arrive and the PA system is switched on. Then you will find the silence filled by the rolling songs of the nightingales that perch in trees beyond the garden boundary. Early morning sunlight illuminates a single rock at the garden's western end, drawing out its rich colours and lighting up enough planes and crevices to absorb your attention and allow the stillness of the place to descend upon you.

RIGHT A weeping cherry throws its branches across the famous shingle-clad clay wall of Ryoan-ji.

OVERLEAF Ryoan-ji's enigmatic garden is made up of fifteen rocks, carefully arranged so that only fourteen of them are visible from any one point. This is thought to reflect the Buddhist belief that the number fifteen denotes completeness, and the difficulty of achieving perfection in this world.

Ryogen-in

There can be no secrets at Ryogen-in, no creeping about at the dead of night, for the nightingale floor overlooking the main garden sings out, its boards creaking and squeaking to advertise every footfall. Garrulous floors of this kind are to be found in many ancient temples, where the carefully sprung boards move up and down, producing their strange chirping by rubbing against the nails that hold them in place. At Ryogen-in the nightingale floor lies on the approach to the *hojo*, or abbot's house, which is surrounded by gardens. They are all dry gardens, *kare-sansui*, designed to be explored by the mind but never entered physically by anyone but the monk whose job it is to prune the plants and rake the gravel into perfect lines or rippling curves.

The oldest and most famous of Ryogen-in's gardens is Ryungintei, an elongated, rectangular space to the north of the *hojo*. This garden was made during the Muromachi era (1393–1568) in *c.* 1504. Moss forms a springy green pelt, covering the ground and lapping against the base of rocks and rounded, topiary shapes. The tall, flat-topped rock at the centre of the garden is said to represent Mount Shumisen, the mountain that Buddhist symbolism places at the core of the universe, and it is surrounded by an ocean of moss and a series of smaller stones that evoke the eight ranks of mountains and seas surrounding Shumisen.

The minuscule A-Un garden lies between the temple and the ochre-coloured, clay perimeter wall. Two rocks barely emerge from the rippled gravel surrounding them. Tiny as they are, and so nearly submerged, they encompass the truth of the universe. One of the rocks represents the syllable 'a', and the other stands for the syllable 'un', and thus they symbolize the complementary opposites at the heart of Zen philosophy, positive and negative, male and female, heaven and earth.

Ryogen-in is part of the Daitoku-ji temple complex. It is one of twenty-three sub-temples, each one enclosed by a wall and surrounded by its own gardens. The views over the clay wall surrounding A-Un are crowded with the exotic rooflines of other temples, trees and garden walls. There are no views from the tiny, enclosed garden of Totekiko, however. It is a minute slip of ground beneath the intersection of two roofs. Two groups of rocks lie in a sea of pale sand, interrupting the flow of parallel lines with spreading pools of circular ripples.

Ishidaan, the garden that flanks the south wall of the *hojo*, was reconstructed in 1980 when a tree that had occupied centre stage for 700 years finally fell down. The current priest designed a new garden, but he chose the ancient legend of the Mystic Isles, where people do not age or die, as his theme. The tallest rock at the back of the garden represents Mount Horai, the largest of the islands. Horai and the other mystical islands were said to float in the sea, suspended on the backs of turtles. Cranes lived there, acting as messengers and providing a convenient means of transport for the islands' immortal inhabitants. It takes a practised eye to recognize the highly abstract crane formed from the rocks to the right of Mount Horai, or the turtle on the grass where the tree once grew at the centre of the garden.

PREVIOUS PAGES
LEFT Ishidaan, a modern garden, was
built in 1980. It was designed by Katsudo,
the abbot of Ryogen-in.

RIGHT ABOVE An ancient camellia,
assiduously pruned, occupies a corner of
Ryugin-tei (the Singing Dragon Garden).

RIGHT BELOW The Isshidan garden at
Ryogen-in, where a mossy island in the
foreground marks the spot where a tree
grew for 700 years. The stones in the
garden represent a crane, a turtle and the
legendary Mystic Isles. The tallest rock at
the far end of the garden represents Mount
Horai, the largest of the Mystic Isles.

ABOVE AND LEFT The tiny garden of
Totekiko at Ryogen-in is said to be the
smallest garden in Japan.

ABOVE Ryugin-tei, the oldest of the five gardens of the Ryogen-in. It is sometimes attributed to the landscape painter Soami, but there is very little evidence to confirm this suggestion.

RIGHT The 'A-un' garden at Ryogen-in. A notice beside it explains that A-un means 'inhale and exhale, heaven and earth, positive and negative, male and female. The garden is designed to display the truth of the universe and the essence of Zen.'

Saiho-ji

There is nothing casual about a visit to the temple of Saiho-ji and its famous garden. First you must make a written request and then await the reply that will give you the time and date of your appointment. All being well, you will catch a bus that carries you beyond the western suburbs of Kyoto to a village on the city's edge, where it deposits you in a small square lined with traditional wooden houses. So far so good, but that is just the beginning. Saiho-ji has always been a crowd puller. By the end of the 1970s there were so many visitors to the garden each day that the abbot felt compelled to close the gates to the general public. Today if you manage to make an appointment, you will be permitted to enter the garden only after attending a special ceremony in the temple, a wonderful experience that becomes more challenging when you are made to attempt an inexpert copy of part of a sacred text, using ink and a surprisingly soft brush.

The garden of Saiho-ji – like Tenryu-ji – is closely associated with Muso Soseki (1275–1351), the fourteenth-century Zen priest, poet, calligrapher, teacher and gardener. Soseki was invited to take over Saiho-ji in 1334. There had been a garden to the east of the temple complex for many centuries. Previous occupants of the site, the Jodo, or 'Pure Land' Buddhists, had excavated the existing ponds. They had created an earthly paradise, a chain of ponds, islands and promontories inspired by beautiful descriptions of Amida Buddha's Western Paradise Garden. By the time Soseki arrived the temple had been badly damaged by a fire and then endured a prolonged period of neglect. The garden was overgrown and virtually derelict.

Soseki converted the temple to Zen Buddhism, changing its name to the Temple of Western Fragrances. He was in his mid-sixties by this time, but he is said to have worked doggedly on the restoration of the ponds and islands in the lower garden. He also built a number of new pavilions and shrines among the trees and on the steep hillside above the garden. It was here, on steeply sloping ground, that Soseki created his *kare-sansui*, a dramatic dry waterfall built across the hillside in *c*.1340 and now the oldest surviving example of a dry garden.

Saiho-ji has a tumultuous history. During the Onin Wars of the mid-fifteenth century the temple complex was burnt to the ground. This seemed to set a pattern for repeated destruction by fire. Two disastrous floods swept through the lower garden and by the mid-nineteenth century the site was abandoned and opportunistic mosses and self-sown trees had begun to creep in. In the early twentieth century the temple was restored, but by now nature had taken its own decisions and defined the character of Saiho-ji's garden. A thick layer of moss has unfolded in the dappled shade of the trees until it covers every inch of the undulating landscape that surrounds the ponds; 120 different varieties of it have been counted, and after the rains of May and June they turn the air itself green with the intensity of their colour. The moss is riddled with streams, some of them no more than a slit in its sleek surface.

Narrow steps link the lower garden to the steep wooded hill above it. The roots of giant cedars, moss clad and monstrously thick, cross a path that disappears between the trees, passing a wooden shrine and winding its way higher and higher until it reaches the famous dry cascade built by Soseki in 1340, making this the oldest surviving example of *kare-sansui*. Here rocks tumble across the slope, looking as if they had been forced into place by a raging torrent, but the pools between them are filled with nothing but moss.

RIGHT In the garden of Saiho-ji, moss
covers the undulating ground between the
trees so thickly and dominates the scene so
entirely that the place has long been known
as *koke-dera* – or the Moss Garden.

BELOW The landscape of Saiho-ji
is complicated by islands, inlets and
promontories that are linked by little bridges
made from logs covered in moss.

BELOW Saiho-ji's mossy carpet is interrupted only by the boundary wall. Moss grows best in damp air and dappled shade, and Saiho-ji provides perfect conditions. The heavy clay soil around the ponds retains water, the site is sheltered from cold north winds and the trees protect the moss from direct sunlight.

RIGHT A gardener at Saiho-ji wears *jika-tabi* – traditional, split-toed boots – and carries a large wicker basket filled with fallen leaves swept from the shining green carpet of moss.

OVERLEAF Saiho-ji may appear to be a very natural garden but this is an illusion. Cultivated moss demands constant attention. It must be kept clean and weeds must be removed by hand. And it is important to tread lightly as you carry out these jobs: moss takes a long time to recover if it is damaged by trampling feet.

Sanzen-in

The bus from Kyoto will set you down in Ohara at the foot of the steep path leading to Sanzen-in. It is lovely to get out into the crisp, country air and climb the hill on a path bordered on one side by a stream and on the other by colourful stalls selling souvenirs, pickled cucumbers on sticks, silk purses and the candied peel of mandarins.

Sanzen-in is a Tendai Buddhist temple originally founded in the tenth century. It has the distinction of being one of the Tendai *monzeki* temples, which means that it has counted members of the imperial family among its abbots. The temple was moved to its present location in 1156, but its two gardens date only from the seventeenth century.

There is a sharp contrast between Sanzen-in's two gardens. The first, known as Shukeki-en, the Garden that Gathers Green, is next to Kyakuden, the reception hall of the temple. The small space is enclosed by a curved hedge on one side and the viewing platform of the temple on the other. A pond fills the foreground, and the slope beyond it is crowded with tightly clipped shrubs and surmounted by a miniature stone pagoda.

The second garden, Yusei-en, the Garden of Pure Presence, lies between the *shinden*, or main hall, and the Ojo-Gokuraku-in, the Amida hall that was originally built in 986 and rebuilt in 1148. The bleached, wooden walls of Ojo-Gokuraku-in can be seen between the fissured, lichen-covered trunks of the Japanese cedars that rise from ground carpeted by a patchwork of different varieties of moss. The small pond is surrounded by maples that flare with brilliant colour in autumn. A statue of the bodhisattva Jizo, one of Japan's most popular gods, stands among the flowering rhododendrons at the edge of the garden. It is most unusual to see a figurative sculpture in a Japanese garden, but at Sanzen-in there are numerous human faces and figures emerging from the moss. Hydrangeas grow densely all over the tree-covered slope above the garden.

RIGHT The Shukeki-en garden (Garden that Gathers Green) next to Sanzen-in's reception hall was redesigned in the early Edo period (1600–1868).

FAR RIGHT
ABOVE
A view across Yusei-en (Garden of Pure Presence) at Sanzen-in. Maples and red cedars surround Ojo Gokuraku-in, the Temple of Rebirth in Paradise.

BELOW The fallen head of a statue appears to emerge from the mossy ground of Yusei-en.

Flowering cherries grow among red
cedars on the hillside above the ancient
Amida hall at Sanzen-in.

A statue of the bodhisattva Jizo
in Sanzen-in's Yusei-en.

103

Shoden-ji

It's a long bus ride from central Kyoto to Shoden-ji in the north-west suburbs of the city. The walk from the bus stop takes you through narrow lanes that cut through the city's market gardens. In spring the fields are densely planted with neat rows of onions and brassicas. The road to the temple climbs steeply through cedars and bamboos, emerging eventually in a sunny clearing where a monk tends the monastery's own vegetable garden.

Shoden-ji was established in 1282 but its garden dates from the early years of the Edo era (1600–1868). It is a *kare-sansui* (dry garden) with a difference. Instead of arranging rocks on the raked gravel below the veranda of the *hojo*, or abbot's house, the designer planted clusters of azaleas. This creates a particularly pleasing contrast between pale gravel raked into perfectly straight lines and the rounded forms of azaleas tightly clipped to create smooth, amorphous shapes that appear to melt into each other. Their immediate backdrop is the flawless, whitewashed surface of the garden wall.

The designer arranged the azaleas just as rocks are arranged in the *kare-sansui* of other temples. The plants grow in clusters of three, five and seven, the auspicious odd numbers that brought harmony to the Zen garden. The clusters grow in volume as well as number from left to right, and this serves to lead the eye across the garden to the decorative gate at the right-hand end of the wall.

Shoden-ji's garden is small, but lift your eyes from the plump contours of the azaleas and you realize that the tile-clad boundary wall is really no boundary at all. The garden seems to extend as far as the horizon, where the view is finally stopped by the magnificent summit of Mount Hiei. *Ikedori*, or 'capturing alive', was the word originally used to describe this technique of borrowing landscape, and it vividly describes the active, potent role that Mount Hiei seems to play in the design of Shoden-ji's garden.

How do you capture a landscape alive? According to Marc P. Keane, himself a landscape architect and the author of several books on the history and design of Japanese gardens, the designers of Japanese gardens borrowed a compositional technique from the artists of the Chinese Sung Dynasty (960–1279). The background of their ink-and-wash landscapes tended to be a majestic natural scene, while the foreground was often made up of tiny figures or minute buildings, a style not unlike that used on the screens inside Shoden-ji's *hojo*. The artist created the perspective in these landscapes by painting a middle ground that would hold the foreground and background of the scene together. It was important that the middle ground did not distract the viewer from the more important elements of the painting, and consequently it was kept deliberately vague. Gardens that make use of *shakkei* employ a similar system to create a link between the garden and a distant landscape feature or building. Shoden-ji is a perfect demonstration of this technique. The garden is the tiny foreground, Mount Hiei is the majestic background and the two are conjoined by unremarkable woods that create a vague and undistracting middle ground. The result of this arrangement is infinitely more dynamic than a simple 'borrowing' of Mount Hiei. It seems to push back the boundaries of the garden and draw the majestic summit of the mountain very much closer to us.

LEFT A lovely decorated bowl containing a few coins stands on the edge of Shishi-no-ko Watashi, Shoden-ji's dry garden.

LEFT A lovely decorated bowl containing a few coins stands on the edge of Shishi-no-ko Watashi, Shoden-ji's dry garden.

BELOW Shoden-ji's beautifully clipped azaleas grow in clumps of three, five and seven plants, an arrangement that mimics that of the rocks in other gardens.

Shosei-en

Shosei-en is a magnificent seventeenth-century stroll garden, a haven for the herons and yellow wagtails that inhabit its pools, streams and pine-clad islands in the heart of modern Kyoto. The garden is part of the Higashihongan-ji temple, although it is separate from the temple complex and was traditionally used as a retreat by the abbot. It is said to have been designed by Ishikawa Jozan (1583–1672) in 1653. In his early life Ishikawa was a solider in the army of the Togukawa clan. He fought many important battles for Togukawa Ieyasu, but eventually fell out with him so badly that he was exiled from Edo (present-day Tokyo). This marked the beginning of a very different phase in his life. He took refuge in Kyoto, and in 1636 he built a beautiful house called Shisen-do and began to create a tiny garden around it. Shisen-do is now a temple, and it is open to visitors.

An extremely high wall encloses the garden, which would be absolutely invisible if it were not for the crowns of the orange trees that arch above the wall and give it away. Shosei-en has always been associated with oranges. Originally there was a grove of *karatachi*, the Japanese bitter orange (*Poncirus trifoliatum*), a near relation of citrus, planted on the garden boundary. These trees, which would have been heavily armed with vicious thorns and covered in tiny orange fruits as bitter as gall, earned Shosei-en the nickname of 'Karatachi-tei'.

The garden is arranged around a series of magnificent ponds. Some people believe that the largest of these was part of a Heian pond garden belonging to Minamoto no Toru (822–95), son of the Emperor Saga. It is not difficult to imagine a Heian boating party taking place on these waters. In *The Tale of the Genji*, written at the beginning of the eleventh century, there is a vivid description of such an event: 'The dragon and phoenix boats were brilliantly decorated in the Chinese fashion. The little pages and helmsmen . . . wore colourful Chinese dress, and everything about the arrangements was deliciously exotic.'

Today the ponds host only herons that crowd on to its rocky islands, managing to look noble and isolated despite the proximity of their neighbours. Koi carp swim so close to the surface that they pull a V-shaped wake through the water. They nose their way into the streams that thread through the garden, and here they pit themselves against the current, their grey backs glistening like muscular stones.

The smaller of the two ponds at Shosei-en is a wonderful lesson in false perspective. Its width diminishes rapidly, creating the impression that the pond is very much longer than it is. This effect is exacerbated by a covered bridge at its far end. It is not until you reach the bridge that you become aware of its miniature proportions – another visual trick that serves to expand the apparent size of the pond.

Shosei-en is richly planted. All the usual suspects are there in abundance: cherries of several different varieties for the spring, water lilies in summer and maples for the autumn. However, the rocky, mossy shores of the ponds are planted with an unusually rich mixture of trees and shrubs, including the Japanese bayberry (*Myrica rubra*), which bears brilliantly coloured, edible fruit. In April, falling cherry blossom billows like a sparse blizzard across the garden. Ishikawa Jozan included poetry among his many skills, sometimes making cherry blossom a melancholy theme:

> Cherry blossoms filling the ground
> Sunset filling my eyes;
> Blossoms vanished, spring old,
> I feel the passing years.
> When blossoms were at their finest I neglected to call.
> The blossoms did not betray me,
> I betrayed the blossoms.

RIGHT A gust of wind scatters cherry blossom over a *Chaenomeles speciosa* 'Nakai' at Shosei-en.

OVERLEAF Herons have colonized an island at Shosei-en, where dwarfed pines grow among the rocks.

LEFT Shinsetsu-kyo, the snow-capped bridge, links the North Island at Shosei-en to the mainland.

BELOW A gentle blizzard of petals covers the ground in fallen cherry blossom at Shosei-en.

RIGHT

ABOVE Shosei-en's paths are carefully designed to weave through the garden, leading the visitor to a series of ideal views. Here an abstract pattern of rock tiles has been set into the path.

BELOW LEFT A staggered stone bridge forces visitors to concentrate as they cross the stream at Shosei-en.

BELOW RIGHT Taka-ishigaki, a highly decorative stone wall that divides the inner and outer gardens at Shosei-in.

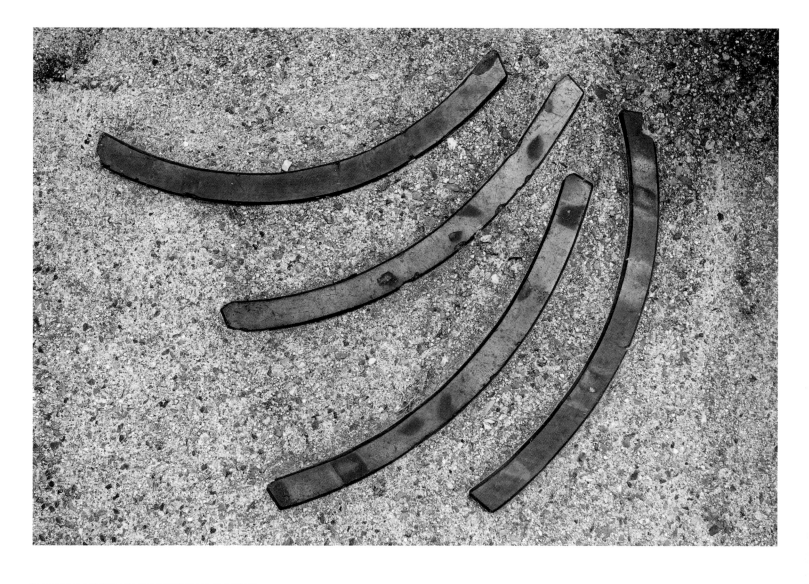

Suizen-ji

Go to Suizen-ji early in the morning, when mist still clings to the water in the vast pond and catches between the contorted branches of the trees. You couldn't invent a landscape stranger than this garden in the middle of Kumamoto, and yet its principal features were all drawn from reality. Suizen-ji is the ultimate example of *shukkei*, the art of creating miniature versions of famous features in the natural landscape. In this case, the garden designer took inspiration from the Tokaida road which linked Kyoto to Edo. This road was of enormous significance to Japan's seventeenth-century *daimyo*, the feudal overlords who were obliged to make regular journeys to Edo, present-day Tokyo, in order to pay their respects to the shogun. Meanwhile, the Emperor of Japan was still in Kyoto, the old capital, and could scarcely be ignored. It's little wonder that Tokaida became the busiest road in Japan. Fifty-three posting inns were established along it and it was the scenery surrounding these important buildings that inspired the designer of Suizen-ji. Two hundred years later, Hiroshige published his famous series of woodblock prints of the same scenes.

In 1632 Hosokawa Tadatoshi, *daimyo* of Higo province, founded the temple of Suizen-ji. Building work on the garden began in 1636, and the temple was later replaced by a tea house. There was already a large pool on the site, fed by the pristine waters of a spring on Mount Aso, an enormous volcano in the centre of Kyushu. Tadatoshi is said to have considered the pool an excellent source of water for making tea.

The 15-acre/6-hectare stroll garden was eighty years in the making. It was finally completed by Tadatoshi's grandson, Hosokawa Tsunatoshi, and renamed Jojuen, or 'garden of elegance', a title that seems to be used interchangeably with Suizen-ji. The site combines all the essential elements of the Edo-era (1600–1868) stroll garden. Three acres/1.25 hectares of it are covered by streams and ponds. The spring-water pool was remodelled to represent Lake Biwa near Kyoto, its shallow waters punctuated by monumental rocks and three islands that are elegantly decorated with clipped and distorted pines, rocks and mounds of azalea. Two of the islands are connected to each other and to the mainland by elegant *sawatari-ishi*, or 'stepping stones in the marsh'. *Tsuki-yama* (artificial hills), another favourite feature of the Edo stroll garden, rise from the east side of the pond. Pine trees are scattered across their sculpted sides, their size carefully controlled and graded so that the tiny trees near the top make the hills look much higher than they really are. The dominant *tsuki-yama*, a wonderful, almost conical shape, represents Mount Fuji.

The Suizen-ji temple was dismantled, but in 1878 a Shinto shrine was built at the northern end of the pond as a memorial to the cultural, moral and intellectual leadership of the Hosokawa family. A Noh theatre was erected on the south side of the garden at the same time as the shrine,and is still used regularly. In 1912 the Kokindenju, a 400-year-old tea house, was brought to Suizen-ji from the garden of Katsura Rikyu in Kyoto (see page 46). The tea house had a special significance for the Hosokawa family, because it was here that Hosokawa Fujitaka, the first Hosokawa *daimyo* (feudal lord), initiated the imperial Prince Toshihito into the ancient art of *waka* poetry.

PREVIOUS PAGES
LEFT Crowds flock to Suizen-ji in spring to enjoy the flowers of the cherry trees that grow all over the garden.

RIGHT ABOVE Mist clings to the water as early-morning sunlight falls on the pond at Suizen-ji. The pond's shape is modelled on that of Lake Biwa in Shiga Prefecture, a familiar sight to the *daimyo* on their regular journeys between Kyoto and Edo.

RIGHT BELOW Suizen-ji is a *tsukiyama teien*, a garden with artificial hills. The most famous of these hills is this miniature version of Mount Fuji.

LEFT The design of this double stone bridge prevents visitors from making a direct approach to the Shinto shrine at the northern end of the pond.

BELOW Suizen-ji's crystal clear ponds are fed continuously with icy spring water that is brought to the garden in underground conduits from Mount Aso, the biggest active volcano in Japan.

RIGHT An elegant stone bridge crosses
the pond at Suizen-ji. Tadatoshi originally
selected this site for a tea house
because it had such a reliable supply of
fresh spring water.

BELOW In 1912 Kokindenju, a
300-year-old tea house, was brought to
Suizen-ji from the garden of Katsura in
Kyoto (see page 46).

Tenju-an

Part stroll garden, part dry garden, the complex landscape surrounding the Tenju-an temple is a garden primer, a garden that has evolved over hundreds of years to encompass features from every period of Japanese garden design. Come here to see carp swimming idly through the ghostly branches of the trees reflected in the pond; come and make your way gingerly across the water on uneven stepping stones, and walk among towering bamboos where camellias have shed waxy, pink petals on the mossy ground. Visit in the autumn if you want to see the rocks in the dry garden set against a blazing backdrop of *Acer palmatum*, or in spring to find irises in flower along the fringes of the ponds and to revel in the exotic, deep-throated song of the Japanese nightingale.

Tenju-an is one of the twelve sub-temples in the vast Nanzen-ji temple complex. The original building on the site was a country villa built in 1267 by the Emperor Kameyama, who later converted it into a Zen temple. In 1336 it was rebuilt by the chief priest of Nanzen-ji, only to be badly damaged during the civil war that reduced so many of Kyoto's temples to ruins in the mid-fifteenth century. The majority of the buildings on the site today date from the end of the sixteenth century.

The garden consists of two main elements. The first is a dry garden to the east of the main hall that was probably laid out when the temple was rebuilt at the beginning of the seventeenth century. It was designed to be seen from the viewing platform outside the main hall. Take off your shoes, settle down on planks made dark and smooth by the passage of untold thousands of sock-clad feet and you find yourself gazing across a pale, rectangular sea of perfectly raked gravel. The feature that marks this garden out from every other is the unusual 'fish-scale' path (*irokojiki*), said to date from the mid-thirteenth century. It runs in a straight line from the viewing platform of the temple, before performing a dramatic dog-leg turn towards the main gate. Its 'scales' are formed from square paving slabs set in a bed of springy, verdant moss to create a pattern of grey-and-green checks that has a shocking, almost revolutionary quality in a landscape from which all other forms of geometry have been banished. An extension to the original path was laid beneath the veranda at the beginning of the seventeenth century. Beyond it, the gravel laps against a string of flat-topped rocks set against a backdrop of trees.

The pond and stroll garden lies beyond the dry garden, to the south of the main hall. It consists of two main ponds that are punctuated by mossy islands and divided by a peninsula, a lovely arrangement that is thought to be part of the original thirteenth-century garden layout. A narrow path leads first to a bridge made from a very distinctive pattern of staggered planks. In early summer a stand of irises on the bank beside the bridge bursts into flower. Visitors to the original garden would instantly have recognized this combination of bridge and flowers as a reference to the *Tale of Ise*, an immensely famous collection of poems written in the tenth century. The image is taken from an episode during a journey made by Ariwara no Narihira, the renowned ninth-century courtier and poet. At one point he and his companions come across a staggered plank bridge with a clump of irises flowering beside it. They are so delighted by the beauty of the flowers that they stop to compose a poem, making each line begin with a syllable from the word for iris. On the other side of the bridge, the air is filled with the sound of a waterfall, and the path meanders along the banks of the ponds and through thickets of towering bamboos interplanted with camellias.

BELOW Brightly coloured carp swim in the pond at Tenju-an.

RIGHT This pine at Tenju-an is reflected in the water of a natural stone basin. The trunk of a pine can be distorted in this way by repeatedly pruning out the leader from the top of the tree.

OVERLEAF
LEFT The sinuous stepping stone bridge leads across one of the two ponds in the lower garden at Tenju-an. It is made either from bridge piers or the bases of pillars that would once have supported a temple.

CENTRE This unusual, fish-scale path leads to a gate that was the original entrance to the grounds of Tenju-an. It is made from a combination of sand, moss and square stones set diagonally across its length.

RIGHT The irises that will flower in early summer are just beginning to appear in the shallow water beside the staggered-plank bridge.

121

Tenryu-ji

On a spring morning there is a holiday mood on the street outside the Tenryu-ji temple complex. Tourists crowd around the brightly coloured shop fronts and the traffic is thrown into chaos by rickshaws that are pulled at breakneck speed by young men. The steep sides of Agashiyama and Kameyama mountains rise beyond the rooftops. Cherry blossom stains their darkly wooded flanks, like bright streaks of quartz running through rocks.

Tenryu-ji was founded in 1339 by Ashigawa Takauji, the first of the Ashigawa shoguns. When Ashigawa Yoshimitsu (1358–1408) set up an official hierarchy of Zen temples in Kyoto, Tenryu-ji joined Shokoku-ji, Kennin-ji, Tofuku-ji and Manju-ji as one of 'the five mountains', or Gozan, which were the most important temples in the city. These state temples became schools for Zen painters and training grounds for government officials and diplomats for the trade with China.

It is generally said that Muso Soseki, one of the most important Zen priests of his age, prompted Ashigawa Takauji to build Tenryu-ji as a place of repose for the spirit of the Emperor Godaigo, whom the shogun had driven into exile when he seized power. Ashigawa Takauji raised the money to build the new temple by reviving trade with China, an action that triggered a tremendous flowering of Zen art in Japan.

Muso Soseki became the abbot of the new temple. It was erected on the site of Kamayama-dono, 'the villa of the turtle mountain', built by Emperor Godaigo's grandfather. The serene pond garden that today lies outside the *hojo*, the abbot's house, was probably part of this original layout, making it one of the oldest gardens in Japan. However, the temple buildings have been burnt down eight times over the centuries. Fire ravaged the site for the last time in 1864, and almost all the existing buildings were erected in its aftermath.

Despite his elevated rank, Muso Soseki lent his own muscle power to the restoration and partial redesign of the garden. Many people criticized and even despised Soseki for getting his hands dirty, but he saw all human activities as a form of spiritual discipline, and made no distinction between the religious and the secular.

Tenryu-ji's garden is a little jewel. The still water of the ponds reflects the cherry blossom and the flowers of the camellias that line their mossy banks. The ponds are small, far too small for boating parties, their layout complicated by tree-clad promontories, islands edged with clipped azaleas, and inlets embroidered with complex compositions of unusually small rocks and spanned by simple stone bridges. The most important feature of the layout is a dry waterfall, known as 'the Dragon gate', that cuts through the steep, shining, moss-clad surface of the hill opposite the *hojo*. Stones tumble down towards the water in a dramatic curve, and two vertical rocks flank the base of the waterfall, where it meets the pond.

Muso Soseki may have designed parts of Tenryu-ji's garden, but nobody attributes this, the garden's core feature, to him. The waterfall and the arrangement of rocks at its base are considered altogether too vertical to be the product of a Japanese mind. This vertical accent is redolent of China and the dramatic ink landscapes of the Sung Dynasty. Some suggest that it may even have been built for the Emperor's grandfather by an emigrant Ch'an Buddhist monk from China. The stone bridges that cross inlets and link the mainland and the tiny islands are also reminiscent of Sung-dynasty landscape paintings.

Paths ascend the hill above the pond garden, climbing through a haze of purple azalea flowers to a magnificent view across the roofs of the temples and sub-temples, across the foaming pink crowns of the cherries, to the mountains that unroll across the skyline.

A view across Sogenchi, Tenryu-ji's
ancient pond, to the cherries and
camellias that flower on the opposite bank.

BELOW One of a series of beautifully framed views through the doors of the *hojo*, or abbot's residence, at Tenryu-ju, towards the wooded slopes of Kamayama.

BELOW LEFT These rocks seem to be half submerged in the mossy ground outside the temple at Tenryu-ji.

BELOW RIGHT This cluster of rocks on the edge of Tenryu-ji's pond suggests a mountainous island with a stone bridge in the foreground and a dry cascade on the hillside just behind it. This composition is generally thought to be the earliest surviving attempt at creating a full-scale landscape in miniature.

OVERLEAF
Weeping cherries, camellias and azaleas create a blazing combination of colours on sloping ground above Tenryu-ji.

LEFT A view across the crowns of the maples that fill the valley below the covered bridge at the entrance to Tofuku-ji.

BELOW The garden that Mire Shigemori laid out on the south side of the hojo at Tofuku-ji in 1939. His design an abstract combination of rocks expressed the simplicity of Zen in the Kamakura period.

To reach Tofuku-ji you must cross Tsutsu-kyo, a covered bridge built high above a stream. This will be your first glimpse of the temple complex. In autumn, its roofs rise from a blazing sea of maples, and in spring the view is filtered through showers of cherry blossom carried on a light wind.

Tofuku-ji is the chief temple of the Tofuku-ji branch of the Rinzai sect of Zen Buddhists. It was originally built between 1236 and 1256 but, like so many of Kyoto's temples, it did not survive long before being burned to the ground. It was rebuilt in the fifteenth century and soon became one of the Kyoto Gozan (the five greatest Zen temples of Kyoto). New sub-temples were added, and soon the complex was the size of a substantial village. In 1880 another fire did its worst, destroying the *hojo*, the abbot's house, and several lesser buildings. The *hojo* building that we see today dates back only to 1889.

There are many sub-temples at Tofuku-ji, and as you walk from the main entrance towards the *hojo* you will pass a series of small, enclosed temple gardens, each beautiful and utterly individual. In some there are trees with pale leaves made from tiny paper prayers that flutter in the wind. The most famous gardens, however, surround the *hojo*. They were designed in 1939 by Mirei Shigemori (1896–1975), who was described by Isamu Noguchi, the renowned Japanese-American artist and landscape designer, as 'a man of tea (reflective tastes), of knowledge (twenty volumes on gardens), and a master garden designer'.

Shigemori, Japan's foremost garden architect during the twentieth century, was invited to design four gardens, one on each side of the *hojo*. The temple was founded during the Kamakura era (1185–1333) and Shigemori sought to combine the simplicity of thirteenth-century design with modern style. The principal garden lies to the south of the building. Here Shigemori chose a very traditional symbolic theme. He made a dry garden, punctuating Hakkai, 'eight rough seas' of swirling gravel, with rocky islands representing Eiju, Horai, Koryo and Hojo, the Isles of the Blest, a consistent theme in the Japanese garden ever since it was first introduced during the Heian era (794–1185). Despite this traditional cargo, Shigemori introduced a modern edge to his design by using rocks with forms that were unusually detailed and exaggerated, shapes that would never have found their way into a traditional *kare-sansui* or dry garden. The rocky islands are made up of a considerable number of stones of contrasting shapes. This crowded effect evokes an image from the 'Secret Teachings on Setting Stones' in *Sakutei-ki*, a seminal textbook on garden design written in the eleventh century. Here large groups of stones are compared to 'a pack of dogs at rest, wild pigs running chaotically, or calves frolicking with their mothers'. Shigemori's stones represent the Isles of the Blest and are therefore static, but the *Sakutei-ki* offers clear instructions for other situations: 'As a rule of thumb, when setting stones, if one pair "flees" from the group, then seven or eight should "chase" after them, like children playing tag.'

At the opposite end of the garden Shigemori created five mossy hillocks to represent the five most important temples in Kyoto during the Kamakura era. A pine is set among these mossy hills, its size checked by meticulous pruning so that it will never outgrow its tiny landscape.

On the northern, western and eastern sides of the building Shigemori stepped away from tradition to create designs that were very much more personal. On the west side he made a pattern from alternating squares of clipped azalea (*Rhododendron obtusum*) and white gravel. It is said that this pattern was inspired by an ancient Chinese method of land division. It is a pity that the azaleas fail to thrive, for their moth-eaten appearance blunts the sharp edges of Shigemori's design. To the north of the *hojo* he continued the chequerboard theme, this time creating much smaller squares from stones set into a bed of moss or gravel. In several places the moss has overflowed its allotted space and it grows raggedly across the stones, undermining once again the crisp edges of the original design. The garden to the east is another *kare-sansui*, although this time the rocks are replaced by recycled bridge-pier foundation stones that have been carefully arranged in the form of the Great Bear. In this instance, we must suppose, the raked gravel surrounding them represents sky, not sea.

RIGHT The garden to the north of Tofuku-ji's *hojo*, where Shigemori took inspiration from ancient Chinese field patterns and set stone squares into a bed of moss.

BELOW The mossy hillocks that Shigemori designed at Tofuku-ji to represent the five most important temples in Kyoto.

Visiting Japanese Gardens

In order to visit Japanese gardens it is not necessary to hire a local guide. With a few exceptions (as indicated below) they can usually be visited without prior appointment. Tourist offices, where English is generally spoken, are also listed here; it is often possible to make an appointment through the local office.

Adachi Museum of Art and Gardens
320 Furukawa-cho, Yasugi-city, Shimane 692-0064
(085) 428 7111

Daichi-ji
Nasaka, Minakuchi-cho, Koka-shi, Shiga 528-0035
(074) 862 0396

Daisen-in
54ñ1 Daitoku-ji-cho, Murasakino, Kita-ku, Kyoto 603-8231
(075) 491 8346

Entsu-ji
38ñ9 Hataeda-cho, Iwakura, Sakyo-ku, Kyoto 606-0015
(075) 781 1875

Ginkaku-ji
2 Ginkaku-ji-cho, Sakyo-ku, Kyoto 606-8402
(075) 771 5725

Heian Jingu
Nishi Tennocho, Okazaki, Sakyou-ku, Kyoto 606-8341
(075) 371 5649

Higashi-Gyoen
1ñ1 Chiyoda, Chiyoda-ku, Tokyo 100-0001
(03) 3213 1111

Hosen-in
187 Shorinin-cho, Ohara, Sakyo-ku, Kyoto 601-1241
(075) 744 2409

Kairaku-en
1ñ3ñ3 Tokiwa-cho, Mito-shi, Ibaraki 310-0033
(029) 244 5454

Katsura Rikyu
Imperial Household Agency Kyoto Office, Kyoto Gyoen Nai, Kamigyo-ku, Kyoto 602-8611
(075) 211 1215
Appointment required: apply with passport to the Imperial Household Agency in Kyotomen Imperial Park, tel (075) 211 1215. For online applications visit http://sankan.kunaicho.go.jp/order/index_EN.htm

Kenroku-en
1ñ4 Kenroku-machi, Kanazawa-shi, Ishikawa 920-0936
(076) 234 3800

Kinkaku-ji
1 Kinkaku-ji-cho, Kita-ku, Kyoto 603-8361
(075) 461 0013

Konchi-in
86ñ12 Fukuchi-cho, Nanzen-ji, Sakyo-ku, Kyoto 606-8435
(075) 771 3511

Koraku-en
1ñ5 Koraku-en, Okayama-shi, Okayama 703-8257

Koto-in
73ñ1 Daitokuji-cho, Murasakino, Kita-ku, Kyoto 603-8231
(075) 492 0068

Murin-an
Nanzenji Kusagawa-cho 31, Sakyo-ku, Kyoto 606-8437
(075) 771 3909

Nanzen-ji Hojo
Fukuji-cho, Sakyo-ku, Kyoto 606-8435
(075) 771 0365

Ritsurin-koen
1ñ20ñ16 Ritsurin-cho, Takamatsu-shi, Kagawa 760-0073
(087) 833 7411

Ryoan-ji
13 Goryoshitano-cho, Ryoan-ji, Ukyo-ku, Kyoto 616-8001
(075) 463 2216

Ryogen-in
82ñ1 Daitokuji-cho, Murasakino, Kita-ku, Kyoto 603-8231
(075) 491 7635

Saiho-ji (also known as Koke-dera)
56 Kamigatani-cho, Matsuo, Nishikyo-ku, Kyoto 615-8286
(075) 391 3631
Appointment required: apply in writing at least four weeks in advance with full details, including the number of visitors and two alternative dates.

Sanzen-in
540 Raigoin-cho, Ohara, Sakyo-ku, Kyoto 601-1242
(075) 744 2531

Shoden-ji
72 Kita Chinjuan-cho, Nishigamo, Kita-ku, Kyoto
(075) 491 3259

Shosei-en
Shichijo-agaru, Karasuma-dori, Shimogyo-ku, Kyoto
(075) 371 9210

Suizen-ji
8ñ1 Suizen-ji-koen, Kumamoto-shi, Kumamoto 862-0956
(096) 383 0074

Tenju-an
Fukuji-cho, Sakyo-ku, Kyoto 606-8435
(075) 771 0365

Tenryu-ji
68 Susukinobaba-cho, Saga, Ukyo-ku, Kyoto 616-8385
(075) 881 1235

Tofuku-ji
778 Honmachi, 15-chome, Higashiyama-ku, Kyoto 605-0981
(075) 561 0087

TOURIST OFFICES

Shimane
665 Asahimachi, Matsue City, Shimane
(085) 521 4034

Shiga
Korabo Shiga 21, 6th floor, 2-1 Uchidehama, Otsu-shi, Shiga
(077) 511 1535

Kyoto
JR Kyoto Station, 2nd Floor
(075) 343 6655

Tokyo
2–8–1 Nishi-Shinjuku, Shinjuku-ku (1st floor of TMG building No. 1)
(03) 5321 3077

Kanazawa
Kinoshinbo-machi, Kanazawa, Ishikawa
(076) 232 5555

Okayama
JR Okayama Station
(086) 222 2912

Kumamoto
JR Kumamoto Station
(096) 352 3743

Select Bibliography

Elizabeth Bibb, *In the Japanese Garden*, Cassell, 1991.

Charles Chesshire, *Japanese Gardening*, Anness Publishing Ltd, 2006.

Lafcadio Hearn, *Glimpses of Unfamiliar Japan*, Kessinger, 2004

Jake Hobson, *Niwaki, Pruning, Training and Shaping Trees the Japanese Way*, Timber Press, 2007.

Thomas Hoover, *Zen Culture*, Random House, USA, 1977.

Marc P. Keane, *The Art of Setting Stones & other writings from the Japanese Garden*, Stone Bridge Press, USA, 2002.

Marc P. Keane, *Japanese Garden Design*, Charles E Tuttle Publishing Co., USA, 1996.

Ran Levy-Yamamori and Gerald Taaffe, *Garden Plants of Japan*, Timber Press, USA, 2004.

Gunter Nitschke, *Japanese Gardens*: *Right Angle and Natural Form*, Taschen, Germany, 1999.

Jiro Takei & Marc P. Keane, *Sakuteiki, Visions of the Japanese Garden*, Tuttle Publishing, 2001.

Teiji Itoh, *Gardens of Japan*, Kodansha Amer Inc., 1998.

Mark Treib and Ron Herman, *The Gardens of Kyoto*, Kodansha International Ltd, Tokyo, 2003.

Acknowledgments

Much of the pleasure of researching and photographing this book came from the kindness and courtesy of the people of Japan. We received a most helpful welcome from gardens, temples and tourist offices in too many places for us to mention them all.

We are particularly grateful to Shinji Nakamura for his invaluable assistance with Japanese correspondence. Among many others, Tomoko Ando at Kenroku-en, Wataru Takeda of the Adachi Museum, Toshiharu Shimizu, Chief Priest of Daichi-Ji, and Shirato Binji at Kairaku-en were especially generous with their time and knowledge; we would like to thank them all.

Index

Page numbers in **bold** type refer to illustrations